The Sacraments and You

The Sacraments and You

by the
Daughters of St. Paul

ST. PAUL EDITIONS

NIHIL OBSTAT:
Rev. Timothy J. Shea
Censor

IMPRIMATUR:
✠ Most Rev. Bernard F. Law, D.D.
Archbishop of Boston

Unless otherwise indicated Scripture texts taken from the Revised Standard Version Bible (RSV) (modified form), Catholic Edition, copyrighted © 1965 and 1966 by the Division of Christian Education of the National Council of the Churches of Christ in the U.S.A., and used by permission.

NOTE: Translation used is indicated each time by:
  * *New American Bible*
  ** *The Jerusalem Bible*

Scripture texts (*) used in this work are taken from the *New American Bible*, copyright © 1970, by the Confraternity of Christian Doctrine, Washington, D.C., and are used by permission of copyright owner. All rights reserved.

Excerpts (**) from *The Jerusalem Bible*, copyright © 1966 by Darton, Longman & Todd, Ltd. and Doubleday and Company, Inc. Used by permission of the publisher.

Excerpts from the English translation of the *Rite of Baptism for Children* © 1969, International Committee on English in the Liturgy, Inc. (ICEL); excerpts from the English translation of *The Roman Missal* © 1973, ICEL; excerpts from the English translation of the *Rite of Anointing and Pastoral Care of the Sick* © 1973, ICEL; excerpts from the English translation of the *Rite of Confirmation* © 1975, ICEL. All rights reserved.

The Sacraments and You has been taken from: *Spiritual Life in the Bible*, © Daughters of St. Paul.

ISBN 0-8198-6866-3

Photo Credits: A. Alvarez — 129
A. Mari — 108
DSP — all others

Copyright © 1985, by the Daughters of St. Paul

Printed in the U.S.A. by the Daughters of St. Paul
50 St. Paul's Ave., Boston, MA 02130

The Daughters of St. Paul are an international congregation of women religious serving the Church with the communications media.

CONTENTS

The Sacrament of Baptism 15
   "Let the Children Come to Me"
   Eternal Life for the Unborn
   What a Human Person Is
   To Live a Christian Life

The Sacrament of Confirmation 31
   The Gift of the Spirit
   Salt of the Earth
   An Inner Force

The Sacrament of Reconciliation 43
   "Whose Sins You Forgive...."
   Confidence in God
   "Let Your Hearts Be Broken...."
   Who Should Go to Confession?
   God Is Eager To Forgive and So
     Is His Church
   Frequent Confession
   Celebrate Penance
   To Grow in Grace

**The Sacrament of the
Holy Eucharist** 67
   The Eucharist as a Sacrament
   Body and Blood of Christ

Faith of the Early Church
What Kind of Bread and Wine?
Our Meeting with Christ
Communion in the Hand
"I Will Give You Rest"
May Our Adoration Never Cease
The Eucharist as a Sacrifice
Pledge of Christ's Immense Love
Belief of First Christians
In the Person of Christ
Changes of Vatican II
He Died for All
The Saving Power of the Mass

The Sacrament of the Anointing of the Sick 105

The Sacrament of Holy Orders 109
St. Paul and Women
A Life for Others

The Sacrament of Holy Matrimony 117
Lasting Love
Parenthood
Children
The Gift of Life
Prayer Insures Fidelity
Prayer

Index 138

You could look at this book
as just another text,
or instead, consider it as...

An Invitation from Jesus the Teacher

When He came to earth and lived among us, Jesus of Nazareth taught us what to *believe* and how to *live*. We can imagine ourselves to be part of that crowd who listened to the Master. Would we have remained just spectators, or would we have become part of the more interested group of disciples? What would *we* have seen in Jesus of Nazareth?

The crowds who watched and listened nearly 2,000 years ago witnessed in action the greatest Teacher who ever lived. We can be tempted to be a little envious of those who listened to Jesus and walked with Him. Yet, do we really have to be envious? Not at all, because we who have been given the gift of faith, and are nourished by the *sacraments*, which are the saving actions of Jesus, have the opportunity of making Him the most important Person in our lives.

The Sacraments and You focuses on the *seven sacraments*, the channels of grace by which Jesus the Master initiates us into, restores and/or increases His life in us. No doubt you have studied the sacraments in other years. But you will find this particular presentation new and, in a way, unique. Why? Because each of the chapters is presented in such a way that you are personally involved in conversation with God the Father, who is your Lord. Let Him speak to you about His Son, Jesus, and *what the sacraments can do in your life.* Jesus wants to touch your mind and heart with the joy of His timeless message, just as He did for the people of the Holy Land nearly 2,000 years ago.

Jesus is offering you the opportunity right now to grow in love for the Father and to listen to His words of love.

With divine patience and goodness, the Divine Teacher awaits your response.

What the Sacraments Can Do!

Just as Jesus the Divine Master gave us the truth to believe—the Gospel message; the way to follow—His law of love; so He also instituted the means to receive His divine life and grow in it—the sacraments. "I came that they may have life," He said, "and have it abundantly" (Jn. 10:10).

The seven sacraments, O God, are the actions of Your Son, Christ, who administers them through men. They are holy because by the power of Christ, they pour grace into the souls of those who receive them. Their purpose is to sanctify us.

Through each of them Christ gives us: His sanctifying grace, that is, a sharing in His divine life; the virtues of faith, hope and charity; the seven gifts of the Holy Spirit—wisdom, understanding, counsel, fortitude, knowledge, piety and fear of the Lord; and special sacramental grace which is the claim to those actual graces which are necessary for the fulfillment of the special purpose of the sacrament.

The Sacrament of Baptism

The Baptism instituted by Your Son, Jesus Christ, was prefigured in the Old Testament by the circumcision (cf. Col. 2:11f.), the march through the Red Sea (cf. 1 Cor. 10:2) and the passage through the Jordan (cf. Jos. 3:14). It was prophesied formally by Your prophet Ezekiel, who spoke in Your name. He said: "I will sprinkle clean water upon you, and you shall be clean from all your uncleannesses, and from all your idols I will cleanse you" (Ez. 36:25).

The baptism given by John the Baptizer was an immediate preparation for the Baptism of Christ. The Johannine baptism did not have the same effective power as the Baptism of Your Son, because it did not confer grace, but only prepared for the reception of grace.

Jesus explained to Nicodemus the nature and necessity of Baptism. He said:

"Truly, truly, I say to you, unless one is born anew, he cannot see the kingdom of God. Truly, truly, I say to you, unless one is born of water and the Spirit, he cannot enter the kingdom of God" (Jn. 3:3, 5).

Before His ascension into heaven, to return to You, His Father, Jesus gave His Apostles the universal mandate to baptize, and directed that they do so in the name of the Father, Son and Holy Spirit (cf. Mt. 28:19).

From the very beginning of the Church, Jesus' Apostles fulfilled the mandate to baptize. In the Acts of the Apostles we read:

"And Peter said to them, 'Repent, and be baptized every one of you in the name of Jesus Christ for the forgiveness of your sins; and you shall receive the gift of the Holy Spirit.' So those who received his word were baptized, and there were added that day about three thousand souls" (Acts 2:38, 41).

Many, O Lord, and priceless are the effects of the sacrament of Baptism:

It brings about the remission of sin, both original sin, and in the case of adults, also all personal mortal or venial sins, provided proper dispositions of faith and sorrow for sin are present. It also confers inner sanctification, by the infusion of sanctifying grace, with which the theological virtues (faith, hope and charity) and cardinal virtues (prudence, justice, fortitude, temperance) and the gifts of the Holy Spirit are always joined. It also effects the remission of all punishments of sin, both the eternal and the temporal, because as St. Paul says, the old man dies and is buried and the new man arises (cf. Rom. 6:3f.).

It is true, Lord, that after Baptism, concupiscence, that is, evil inclinations, remain, as well as suffering and death. However, their purpose is not to be a punishment but a means of testing our union with Christ.

Moreover, Baptism imprints in the soul of the recipient an indelible spiritual mark—the baptismal character. Because of this sacramental character the baptized person is incorporated into the Mystical Body of Christ, which is the Catholic Church. Therefore, he becomes a member of this one, holy, catholic and apostolic Church, founded by Your Son, our Savior, to continue His mission of salvation throughout the centuries until the end of time.

The baptismal character is a consecration of the baptized to Christ, and it makes him participate in Christ's priestly role, as St. Peter writes: "You are a chosen race, a royal priesthood, a holy nation, God's own people, that you may declare the wonderful deeds of him who called you out of darkness into his marvelous light" (1 Pt. 2:9).

We hear today so many people boasting about being "born-again Christians." With this some mean that they have received a "new baptism." Do they not know, O Lord, that there is no validity in a second baptism, due to the fact that Baptism imprints a *lasting* character and therefore can be received only once? Once one is baptized, he is a Christian forever!

"Let the Children Come to Me"

For the sake of eternal salvation, even infants should be baptized. Jesus says: "Let the children come to me, and do not hinder them; for to such belongs the kingdom of heaven" (Mt. 19:14). And again: "Truly, truly, I say to you, unless one is born of water and the Spirit, he cannot enter the kingdom of God" (Jn. 3:5).

Children were baptized from the beginning of Your Church. This practice is attested by St. Irenaeus, Tertullian, St. Hippolitus of Rome, Origen, and St. Cyprian. Origen establishes the importance of child Baptism by reason of the presence of original sin, and he attests that this practice dates back to the Apostles.

In Your Book, O God, we repeatedly read of the Baptism given to an entire "household." This means that any children in the family were included. This is all the more understandable when we recall that Christian Baptism replaced circumcision, which was performed soon after birth (cf. 1 Cor. 1:16; Acts 11:14; 16:15, 33; 18:8).

O God, may all parents understand that Your mercy and grace should not be refused to any child. Baptism is too necessary to postpone it. The life of a child is fragile, as if suspended by a slender thread which can be severed by the least unfortunate happening.

St. Teresa of Avila visited often with her sister, Joan of Ahumada. When she learned of the birth of a little nephew, the saint wanted him to be baptized right away and given the name Joseph, since she was greatly devoted to this saint. After the child was baptized, she took him in her arms and said, "I pray God that if one day you should turn away from Him, He take you while you are still like a little angel, before you offend Him."

Three weeks later, the baby boy became gravely ill. The saint again took him in her arms and looked into his face intently. Her own face became as beautiful as an angel's. At that moment the baby died.

The saint wanted to leave, but in her grief her sister said, "Don't go away! Look, my little

Joseph is dead!" St. Teresa revealed what she had seen in that moment in which she looked in the infant's face: "We have a great motive for praising God!" she said. "I saw a multitude of angels who welcomed the soul of this little one, who resembled them."

Even though in the early Church the administration of Baptism was regarded as a privilege of the bishop, we read in Your Bible that this mandate to baptize, addressed to the Apostles (cf. Mt. 28:19), was transferred by them to others. The Acts of the Apostles records: "He (the eunuch) commanded the chariot to stop, and they both went down into the water, Philip and the eunuch, and he (Philip the deacon) baptized him" (Acts 8:38).

Provided it is correctly administered, according to the form laid down by Your Church, anyone can validly baptize. In case of necessity, this sacrament can be administered by a lay man or woman, even by a pagan or heretic, as long as the minister adheres to the form of the Church (pouring, sprinkling or immersing in water of the person to be baptized, while the formula, "I baptize you in the name of the Father, and of the Son, and of the Holy Spirit" is said) and has the intention of doing what the Church does. The intrinsic reason for the validity of Baptism administered by anyone is that the sacrament is necessary for salvation, as Your Son made clear.

Eternal Life for the Unborn

What is to be said, O Lord, of the horrible crime of abortion, which deprives millions of children of temporal life and also of the life of grace received in Baptism? Let us read the comments of Father Bertrand de Margerie, S.J., a contemporary theologian, in regard to the baptism of aborted fetuses:

"In the last analysis, it is a question, through the right of the victims of abortion to eternal life, of recognizing the right of Christ Jesus, their Creator, Redeemer, the author and principal minister of Baptism, to baptize and incorporate in His Church these children condemned to death by their mothers and their doctors. Did He not shed His infinitely precious blood for them? Not in the first place and mainly for their temporal salvation, itself mortal, but for their eternal salvation. He, too, in the first place, suffered an unjust death in order that these children might be admitted to the beatific vision in as guaranteed a way as possible.

"Recently a nurse in a French hospital told me that she had, with the consent of the mother, baptized an aborted fetus that was still alive.

"Is it a question, as some believe, of an action which has become obsolete since Vatican II? Or, is it a question of an action which, pastorally, is useless—one not to imitate and especially one not to propose as an example?

"If it is true that Almighty God, in His wisdom and infinite mercy, can, if He wills it, introduce into the vision of His perfections, in consideration of the merits of Christ and of His Church, an infant who died without Baptism before the age of reason, it is fitting to recall that this consoling view represents a simple conjecture which the Church at no moment of its history has wanted to guarantee. No document of Vatican II nor any official and post-conciliar text of the Church has come to change the traditional doctrine of the Church recalled by Pius XII in his discourse to midwives on October 29, 1951: after the promulgation of the Gospel, the sacramental Baptism of water (cf. Jn. 3:5-6) is the only sure means of eternal salvation for human beings who die before the age of reason....

"Hence it follows that Catholic moral theology, including its post-conciliar publications, always recognizes the grave obligation on the part of those who have charge of infants to have the infant baptized if it is in danger of death. The reason is that the Church cannot toy with the security of man's eternal salvation, and that is why she has also established canonical legislation touching this point. Canon law still holds good, as Paul VI recalled.

"It should not be difficult to believe that an age, which is so rightfully preoccupied with social security when it is a matter of employment, of revenues, and of life in this world, is also qualified to understand that the Church is passionately concerned with providing a surer way to eternal life, especially for the weakest of children. Thus Canon 750, in the old Code of Canon Law as well as in the project of the new Code, merely translates in juridical terms this basic principle of Catholic moral theology: one must help one's neighbor who finds himself in extreme spiritual need even at the peril of one's own life (cf. 1 Jn. 3:16).

"...From the point of view of the child's well-being too often forgotten, how can one, for any motive whatsoever, sacrifice a human being's inalienable right to a secure place in eternity as a beholder and adorer of the living God? If one does not succeed in saving his temporal life, is there a reason for sacrificing his right to be baptized or his right to attain eternal life in an unmistakable manner?

"In fact, we think that many nurses, if these views were presented to them, would be happy to contribute directly to the eternal salvation of these little personally innocent beings, and so sometimes, in raising this question, even to contribute to their temporal safety."

This sacrament, Lord, is so indispensable for salvation that in a case of emergency, the Baptism by water can be replaced by Baptism of desire (an explicit or implicit desire for sacramental Baptism, united with perfect sorrow for sins) or Baptism by blood (martyrdom of an unbaptized person by reason of his confession of the Christian Faith or practice of Christian virtue).

In regard to the Baptism of blood, Jesus attests: "Every one who acknowledges me before men, I also will acknowledge before my Father who is in heaven.... He who finds his life will lose it, and he who loses his life for my sake will find it" (Mt. 10:32, 39).

And again: "He who loves his life loses it, and he who hates his life in this world will keep it for eternal life" (Jn. 12:25).

What a Human Person Is

A young man remarked to his philosophy professor: "As for me, I consider a fetus no more human than a fish. Those who are retarded or old and useless are not persons either in my opinion. One becomes a person only when he is free to do what he wants and able to go ahead in life without regard for law or authority to reach his own individual goals."

Lord, such a way of reasoning is only possible in our day because our young people are instructed in such erroneous positions. Due to their philosophical and psychological background, they are probably not completely responsible for their wrong outlook.

Our purpose here is to speak of what a person *really is*. After all, this is in place here, since we've just considered the reasons for baptizing an aborted fetus, still alive; or, an infant, that has not yet attained the use of reason; or, the retarded. In addition, the consideration of what a person is preserves us from the crime of euthanasia, by which old persons or those considered "unuseful" are eliminated.

It is because of wrong concepts that wrong conclusions are reached. In this case, it is the false idea of what a person *is* that leads to evils such as abortion, infanticide and euthanasia.

Biological terms, familiar to everyone, are useful in clarifying the truth:

A person does not belong to the *inanimate kingdom* of rocks and minerals, and all those things in nature which have no life.

Nor does a person belong to the *plant kingdom*. In this kingdom are included, for example, trees, grass and flowers. These are living creatures because they have the power of growth, of which their material soul is the principle. This soul has only vegetative powers, and is transmitted by the parent plants.

Nor does a person belong to the *animal kingdom*. Even though people classify horses and dogs among the most "knowing" of animals, they have only *sense knowledge*, which is essentially different from man's intellectual knowledge. In fact, if a dog were to find a hundred-dollar bill on the ground, it would mean no more to him than a scrap of paper blown from a trash container.

Animals can never go beyond their exterior and interior senses. Their sense knowledge or sensitive power is instinctive, not intellectual. The life principle or the animal "soul" is material, transmitted through generation. While it is one and permeates all parts of the animal's body, and has the powers of growth, movement and sense knowledge, the life principle or animal "soul" dies with the body.

How appropriate here, Lord, is the story of a little country girl who looked intently at the corpse of a cow. As she stared, she felt very sorry for it, because, she said, "It's *all* dead, *all* dead."

Yet, Lord, how many hospitals are there to care for animals while they are living, when they are sick. And there are even cemeteries set aside for them after their death. Just last summer I saw one such cemetery near an institute of higher education. There the students stop to read gravestone inscriptions with the horses' names and the dates marking their birth and death....

On the other hand, men and women—persons—belong to the human kingdom. When You Yourself created man, You said these words recorded in Your Bible: "Let us make man in our image, after our likeness..." (Gn. 1:26). This means that the person is distinguished from the inanimate, plant and animal kingdoms because of the different nature of his soul.

The nature of the human soul, contrary to the nature of the plant or animal life principle, is *spiritual,* and it is at once the principle of vegetative, sensitive and intellectual activity. One proof of the spirituality of the human soul is the power of man to invent. Unlike animals who are only able to retain images they have received through their senses, man is able, through his intellect, to use the material that his senses convey to his brain in such a way as to form or create thoughts or ideas. Furthermore, the mind of man is able to develop new ideas. This ability accounts for the ever-increasing number of inventions and the astounding progress made in all fields.

The soul is active throughout the human body. Since it is spiritual—that is, without parts—it cannot wear out, decay or corrupt. Thus, at death it is the body which dies, not the soul. Death occurs when the soul has left the body.

A Humorous Story

In treating of the spirituality of the soul, a humorous story comes to mind. A renowned military officer said to one of his "simple" subjects, who believed in the spiritual soul: "I do not believe in anything which cannot be seen."

"Well then, sir," the soldier retorted, "I should not believe you have an intelligence because I cannot see it!" Needless to say, the officer made no further remark.

Coming back to our student who believes that a fetus is no more human than a fish; and, that the retarded and the aged and infirm are not persons, we conclude by restating what we have demonstrated here: all of these are indeed persons, whose nature includes a spiritual soul and a human body, and that the soul is at once the principle of vegetative, sensitive and intellectual activity.

In all stages of life—from the moment of generation to the moment of death—a human being is a person because, the life principle of his human nature, that is, his human soul is already *one*, spiritual and immortal. It is because of his soul that the fetus grows; the infant shows a sensitive knowledge; and later at about seven years of age—when the body is more developed in all its parts, thus becoming a fitting tool for the soul—the child is able to reason. Greater development comes with further growth, experience, study, reflection and application.

What of the retarded, mentally disabled or the impaired aged? Because of physical disorder—incurred by a brain hemorrhage, for example—they are hindered in the full *exercise* of the intellectual power of the soul. However, they are not lacking the power itself. They are persons because each has one soul and this soul is human.

Such stress on the person is so important in our day, O Lord. And this emphasis is pleasing to You, for You want us to obey Your command: "You shall not kill."

To Live a Christian Life

Lord, while this most important sacrament, which opens the door to the other sacraments, bestows on the recipient so many valuable gifts, it also imposes the obligation to live according to the Christian way of life. In fact, the person who receives Baptism, thus becoming a Christian, obliges himself to profess his faith (the doctrine of Jesus Christ) and to keep His law (the Ten Commandments, as confirmed and perfected by Your Son). Therefore, he renounces all that is opposed to this, that is, sins against the Faith or the Commandments.

To believe and live as Christians, we are given in Baptism the supernatural virtues of faith, hope and charity.

Meaningful are the baptismal promises:

Do you reject Satan?
I do.

And all his works?
I do.

And all his empty promises?
I do.

Do you believe in God, the Father almighty, Creator of heaven and earth?
I do.

Do you believe in Jesus Christ, His only Son, our Lord, who was born of the Virgin Mary, was crucified, died, and was buried, rose from the dead, and is now seated at the right hand of the Father?
I do.

Do you believe in the Holy Spirit, the holy Catholic Church, the communion of saints, the forgiveness of sins, the resurrection of the body, and life everlasting?
I do. *Rite of Baptism for Children*

This is the Christian Faith which You gave to us, O God, and we are proud to profess it.

Yes, Father, in our era of religious confusion some of Your children abandon Your Church under the pretext that in other churches they find Your word, the Bible. But is not the Bible read and explained with the assistance of Your Holy Spirit in the Church founded by Your Son? And what about the renunciation by these people of the means of grace which You gave Your Church—the seven sacraments? Should they wish to know if they are right in acting thus, for their own sake they should be told the truth: it is never permissible to leave the Catholic Church for any reason whatsoever.

O God, all-powerful Father of Jesus Christ our Lord, You have given us a new birth by water and the Holy Spirit, and forgiven all our sins.

May You also keep us faithful to our Lord Jesus Christ for ever and ever. Amen.

Knowing the weakness of human nature, Your Son provided another sacrament—Confirmation—in which He gives to us the special strength of the Holy Spirit. Through it we are made courageous in professing our faith, we are strengthened to battle against the enemies of our salvation (our passions, the devil, the spirit of the world), and we are fortified in spreading the Faith by word and deed.

The baptismal promises now precede the reception of this sacrament, so the close connection of Confirmation with Baptism is better seen.

Already the prophets of the Old Testament had foretold of the outpouring of Your Holy Spirit over the whole of humanity as a characteristic of the Messianic era (cf. Joel 2:28f.; Is. 44:3-5; Ez. 39:29).

Your Son Jesus had promised His disciples that the Holy Spirit would be sent to them by the Father and by Him, to perfect the grace of Baptism and to help them to bear fearless witness to their faith, even before persecutors. He said:

"When they bring you before the synagogues and the rulers and the authorities, do not be anxious how or what you are to answer or what you are to say; for the Holy Spirit will teach you in that very hour what you ought to say" (Lk. 12:11-12).

The day before Your Son suffered, He assured His Apostles that He would send the Spirit of truth from You, O Father: "When the Counselor comes, whom I shall send to you from the Father, even the Spirit of truth, who proceeds from the Father, he will bear witness to me..." (Jn. 15:26). The Spirit would remain with them forever: "I will pray the Father, and he will give you another Counselor, to be with you for ever" (Jn. 14:16). He would help them to be Christ's witnesses (cf. Jn. 15:26).

On the day of the feast of Pentecost; Jesus did in fact keep His promise. The Holy Spirit came down upon the Apostles, gathered together in the Cenacle with Mary the Mother of Jesus, and a group of the disciples. Your book tells us that they were so filled with the Holy Spirit that they immediately began to proclaim Your mighty works, O God. We read: "They were all filled with the Holy Spirit and began to speak in other tongues, as the Spirit gave them utterance" (Acts 2:4). It was then that Peter recognized the Holy Spirit as the Gift of the Messianic Age. We read:

"Peter, standing with the eleven, lifted up his voice and addressed them, 'Men of Judea and all who dwell in Jerusalem, let this be known to you, and give ear to my words.... This is what was spoken by the prophet Joel:
"And in the last days it shall be, God declares,
   that I will pour out my Spirit upon all flesh,
   and your sons and your daughters shall
     prophesy,
   and your young men shall see visions,
   and your old men shall dream dreams;
yes, and on my menservants and my maidser-
   vants in those days

I will pour out my Spirit; and they shall
  prophesy' ' " (Acts 2:14, 16-18).

Thus, those who believed the Apostles' preaching were baptized and also received the gift of the Holy Spirit. Again the Acts of the Apostles records:

"Peter said to them, 'Repent, and be baptized every one of you in the name of Jesus Christ for the forgiveness of your sins; and you shall receive the gift of the Holy Spirit' " (Acts 2:38).

The Gift of the Spirit

From that time on the Apostles, in accord with the desire of Your divine Son, imparted the Gift of the Spirit to the newly baptized by the laying on of hands. In the Acts of the Apostles we read: "Now when the apostles at Jerusalem heard that Samaria had received the word of God, they sent to them Peter and John, who came down and prayed for them that they might receive the Holy Spirit; for it had not yet fallen on any of them, but they had only been baptized in the name of the Lord Jesus. Then they laid their hands on them and they received the Holy Spirit" (Acts 8:14-17).

In regard to this passage, St. Cyprian (third century) says: "This still happens in our community. Those who are baptized in the Church are brought before the overseers of the Church (bishops) and by our prayer and our imposition of hands receive the Holy Spirit, and by the zeal of the Lord they are perfected."

Together with laying his hand upon each of the candidates, the bishop anoints the foreheads

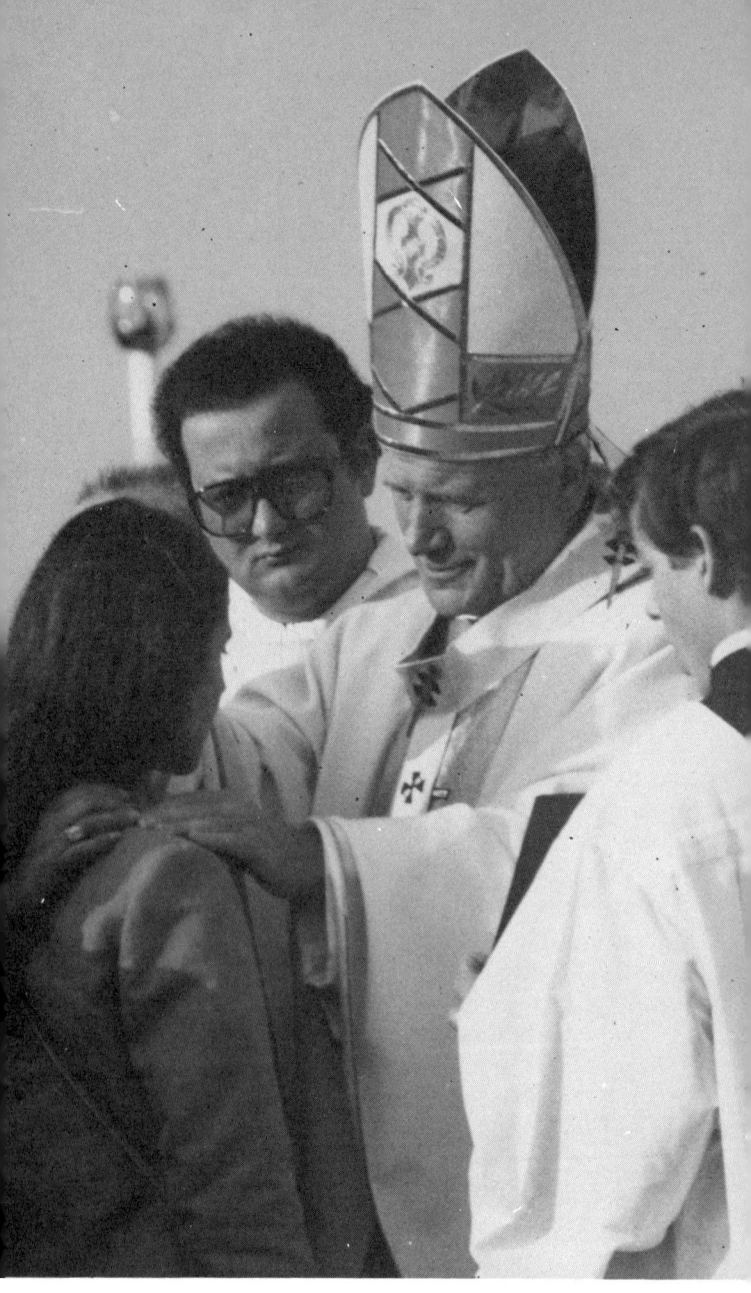

of those to be confirmed with chrism in the form of a cross, while he says: "N., be sealed with the Gift of the Holy Spirit." *Rite of Confirmation*

This is in fulfillment of Jesus' promise to send His Holy Spirit not only upon His Apostles, but also to all His future followers: " 'He who believes in me, as the scripture has said, "Out of his heart shall flow rivers of living water." ' Now this he said about the Spirit, which those who believed in him were to receive; for as yet the Spirit had not been given, because Jesus was not yet glorified" (Jn. 7:38-39).

In the sacrament of Confirmation, the Holy Spirit, already present in the soul of the baptized, together with You, O Father, and Your Son, takes up His abode in the soul of the recipient in a new and supernatural manner. Thus, the Holy Spirit endows the soul with a special strength and joins the confirmed to You in a closer supernatural union, by means of sanctifying grace, the theological and cardinal virtues, and the abundance of His gifts and fruits of joy, peace, patience, kindness, goodness, longanimity, humility, fidelity, modesty, continence and chastity.

Confirmation also imprints on the soul an *indelible* spiritual mark, or character, and for this reason the sacrament cannot be repeated. This seal, as the character received in Baptism, cannot be erased for all eternity. Moreover, because of the character received in this sacrament, the Christian is bound more perfectly to the Church and is enriched with a special strength of the Holy Spirit so that he may live in the world as a witness of Christ.

Salt of the Earth

Speaking to the laity, John Paul II says: "I would like to speak to you about that special dignity and mission entrusted to the lay people in the Church. St. Peter says that Christians are 'a royal priesthood, a holy nation' (1 Pt. 2:9). All Christians, incorporated into Christ and His Church by Baptism, are consecrated to God. They are called to profess the faith which they have received. By the sacrament of Confirmation, they are further endowed by the Holy Spirit with special strength to be witnesses of Christ and sharers in His mission of salvation. Every lay Christian is therefore an extraordinary work of God's grace and is called to the heights of holiness. Sometimes, lay men and women do not seem to appreciate to the full the dignity and the vocation that is theirs as lay people. No, there is no such thing as an 'ordinary layman,' for all of you have been called to conversion through the death and resurrection of Jesus Christ. As God's holy people you are called to fulfill your role in the evangelization of the world.

"Yes, the laity are 'a chosen race, a royal priesthood,' also called to be 'the salt of the earth' and 'the light of the world.' It is their specific vocation and mission to express the Gospel in their lives and thereby to insert the Gospel as a leaven into the reality of the world in which they live and work. The great forces which shape the world—politics, the mass media, science, technology, culture, education, industry and work—are precisely the areas where lay people are especially competent to exercise their mission. If these forces are guided by people who are true disciples of Christ, and who are, at the same time, fully competent in the relevant secular knowledge and skill, then indeed will the world be transformed from within by Christ's redeeming power."

Among other speakers at a convention for lay men and women were a college president, a lawyer and a young professor. They spoke with such orthodoxy, conviction and enthusiasm that one could not help but reflect, "Yes, Lord, there are still many good people."

These three men do not enjoy great renown, but they are certainly genuine lay apostles, acting as leaven in the midst of society. Their message was to remind their listeners of the duty of a Christian to be the "odor of Christ," to witness to the goodness and holiness of the Lord in whatever his or her walk of life.

How convincing they were because they themselves are *doers* of the word and not merely talkers, as St. James has said (cf. Jas. 1:22). And thus the gifts and fruits of the Holy Spirit received in Confirmation were very much at work in them. Dedication to their good-sized families and their students and clients is their way of using these divine gifts.

Impressive was the message which the college president gave in his ex-army-commander tone:

"At the start of changes in the Church after Vatican II I began, as so many others, to complain. My comments were directed against all those I considered responsible, including bishops, priests and religious. I was so upset that I could not even sleep at night, thinking of what was going on. I became not only frustrated, but increasingly angry.

"Yet my conscience was not in peace. I soon realized that I was going nowhere with this type of attitude. It was then that I remembered what the good Sisters had taught me in Catholic school, 'Pray to solve problems!'

"So I changed directions. With prayer, good ideas came of how to help the situation. I began writing articles for newspapers and magazines—positive articles aimed at rebuilding, not destroying through criticism. I also gave lectures encouraging people to do the same, and I have joined a movement dedicated to encouraging this type of positive approach. Now my conscience is at peace and I am convinced that if we all do our part, things will work out for the best. We can do good no matter what our walk of life, and if we do, the world will be a little better because of us." A thunderous applause arose. But before returning to his seat in his humble but dignified manner, he called attention to the statement of Vatican II in *Lumen gentium* about the apostolate of the laity:

"The supreme and eternal Priest, Christ Jesus, since He wills to continue His witness and service also through the laity, vivifies them in His Spirit and increasingly urges them on to every good and perfect work.

"For besides intimately linking them to His life and His mission, He also gives them a sharing in His priestly function of offering spiritual worship for the glory of God and the salvation of men. For this reason the laity, dedicated to Christ and anointed by the Holy Spirit, are marvelously called and wonderfully prepared so that ever more abundant fruits of the Spirit may be produced in them. For all their works, prayers and apostolic endeavors, their ordinary married and family life, their daily occupations, their physical and mental relaxation, if carried out in the Spirit, and even the hardships of life, if patiently borne—all these become 'spiritual sacrifices acceptable to God through Jesus Christ' (1 Pt. 2:5). Together with the offering of the Lord's body, they are most fittingly offered in the celebration of the Eucharist. Thus, as those everywhere who adore in holy activity, the laity consecrate the world itself to God" (no. 34).

An Inner Force

If we are going to witness to our belief in Christ and His teachings, for which Your sacrament of Confirmation prepares us, we must know the content and live it. Contrary to a very widespread opinion, O Lord, we know that the obligation to continue learning about our religion even after the reception of Confirmation is not to be lightly neglected.

In this sacrament, too, O God, You provide the confirmed with those actual graces necessary to fulfill his or her duties as a confirmed Catholic.

There are many temptations which today afflict Your people, O God. Difficulties continually arise, often leading to discouragement. The Evil One always strives to extinguish the light of confidence in the hearts of young people in particular, as well as adults.

May we be aware that we possess an inner force, communicated to us especially in the sacrament of Confirmation. With this hope in Christ's grace we can be optimistic and even joyful.

May we, therefore, be intrepid witnesses to the risen Christ and never retreat before the obstacles we meet with along the path of our lives. Grant us, O Lord, the grace of fortitude and optimism.

O Lord, it is wonderful that in our day and because of Vatican II, devotion to the Holy Spirit, who was once called "the forgotten God," is renewed—and rightly so.

Your Son is the one who sent the Holy Spirit to us to be our Sanctifier. And He works especially through the sacraments. He is the same Spirit You gave to Your Church, to be with her as the Spirit of Truth, protecting her from teaching in matters of faith and morals anything else but the truth, that truth which You Yourself first taught.

However, there are today within the Catholic Church and throughout the world what could be termed "little churches" or "covenant communities," made up of groups of Catholics who call themselves charismatics and pentecostals. They profess a great devotion to the Holy Spirit, but, as we are informed by honest theologians, who, with the passing of years, look more and more into this movement, some of these Catholics seem to lose, little by little, their total identity. The fact is, as experience affirms, that some of the members emerge from these groups damaged psychologically and spiritually.

O God, may Your Holy Spirit be recognized by them as He is—*One* God and only one, the same Holy Spirit Your Son gave to the Church He founded, the Spirit of Truth, in whom there cannot be any contradiction. And may these Catholics, who because of their baptism belong to the holy Catholic Church, which is the Mystical Body of Christ, be faithful to her by being united in the Holy Spirit, in the same faith, the same sacraments, and the same government.

When in these new movements doctrines concerning the Church especially are no longer according to Your teachings about her nature and mission, it is not surprising that the followers may sooner or later be tempted to abandon it.

May the Holy Spirit enlighten us all so that we will repeat with Peter to Jesus when He asked, "Will you also go away?" and he answered emphatically, "Lord, to whom shall we go? You have the words of eternal life..." (Jn. 6:67-68).

The Sacrament of Reconciliation

We read in the Old Testament of how often the prophets invited men to repentance.

When John the Baptizer, the last and greatest prophet, came, he too preached a baptism of repentance for the forgiveness of sins. The evangelist records:

"...John the Baptist appeared in the wilderness, proclaiming a baptism of repentance for the forgiveness of sins" (Mk. 1:4).**

Jesus Himself started His mission by preaching repentance. He said: "Repent, and believe the Good News" (Mk. 1:15).** Your Son not only exhorted men to repentance but also welcomed repentant sinners and reconciled them with You. And since the life of Christians here on earth is a battle, subject to temptations and sins, Your divine Son, our Savior, opened for us the way of the Sacrament of Reconciliation (or Penance), so that we may obtain pardon from You, our merciful Father, and reconcile ourselves with the Church.

Jesus said to Peter: "I will give you the keys of the kingdom of heaven..." (Mt. 16:19).**

In ancient times, giving the keys of a city meant recognizing the authority of the receiver over it. With these words Jesus meant to give to Peter, the head of His Church, supreme authority on earth over Your kingdom, O God. As the one who possessed the keys of a town or city has full power to allow entrance to a person or exclude him, so is the Church empowered with regard to a person who has committed mortal sin, which hinders him from entering the kingdom of heaven. St. Paul says:

"You can be quite certain that nobody who actually indulges in fornication or impurity or promiscuity—which is worshiping a false god—can inherit anything of the kingdom of God" (Eph. 5:5).**

Thus, the power to forgive sins must also be included in the power of the keys. Your prophet Isaiah said:

"I place the key of the House of David
on his shoulder;
should he open, no one shall close,
should he close, no one shall open"
(Is. 22:22).**

Immediately after the promise of the power of the keys, Jesus said to St. Peter:

"...Whatever you bind on earth shall be considered bound in heaven; whatever you loose on earth shall be considered loosed in heaven" (Mt. 16:19).**

In the language of the time, these words, *binding* and *loosing* meant a judgment as to the permissibility or non-permissibility of an action. They also meant the exclusion from the community by the imposition of a ban, or the reacceptance by removal of a ban. Therefore, because sin is the reason for the exclusion, the power to forgive sins is included in the power of binding and loosing.

Besides Peter, Jesus also promised the power of binding and loosing to the other Apostles. Speaking to them Jesus said:

"I tell you solemnly, whatever you bind on earth shall be considered bound in heaven; whatever you loose on earth shall be considered loosed in heaven" (Mt. 18:18).**

On Sunday evening, the day of His resurrection, Jesus fulfilled His promise. He appeared to His Apostles in the locked room, greeted them with a salutation of peace, and showed them His hands and His side to reassure them of His resurrection. Then He transferred to the Apostles the mission which He Himself had received from You, O Father, "to seek and to save that which was lost" (cf. Lk. 19:10),** a mission which He had fulfilled upon earth. The Gospel records many examples, among them that of the man afflicted with palsy:

"Some people appeared, bringing him a paralytic stretched out on a bed. Seeing their faith, Jesus said to the paralytic, 'Courage, my child, your sins are forgiven' " (Mt. 9:2).**

And another example is the public sinner:

"...I tell you, her sins, which are many, are forgiven" (Lk. 7:47).

Jesus invested His Apostles with the same power, as St. John testifies in his Gospel:

Jesus said:
" 'As the Father sent me,
so am I sending you.'
After saying this he breathed on them and said:
'Receive the Holy Spirit.
For those whose sins you forgive,
they are forgiven;
for those whose sins you retain,
they are retained' " (Jn. 20:21-23).**

O God of mercy, this is not a mere covering of sin, but is actual forgiveness on Your part of our sins, an eradication of them, as St. John says:

"...God who is faithful and just
will forgive our sins and purify us
from everything that is wrong" (1 Jn. 1:9).**

In his address to the people at the Temple of Jerusalem, Peter spoke these words:

"You must repent and turn to God, so that your sins may be wiped out..." (Acts 3:19).**

The power of forgiving sins was not a personal gift, but was to be passed on by the Apostles to their successors, just like the powers of preaching, baptizing, and celebrating the Eucharist were to be. The reality of sin makes a continuation of this power necessary for all times.

"Whose Sins You Forgive..."

In the sacrament of Reconciliation or Penance, sins are truly and immediately remitted (cf. Jn. 20:23) by You, O God, through Your ministers, the bishops and priests. They are the *sole* possessors of the power of absolution because Your Son promised this power to the Apostles *only* (cf. Mt. 18:18) and transferred it to them only (Jn. 20:23). From the Apostles it was passed on to their successors in the priesthood, that is, the bishops and the presbyters.

St. Cyprian testifies that the forgiveness of sins and the giving of the peace of the Church took place "through the priests."

St. Ambrose says: "This right is given to the priests only." St. Leo I remarks that the forgiveness of sins in the sacrament of Penance can only be obtained by the prayers of the priest.

St. John Chrysostom wrote: "Our priests received the power not merely of declaring an unclean soul instead of a leprous body to be clean (as the Jewish priests had the power to declare those cleansed from leprosy to be clean...). Our priests instead received the power of entirely purifying the soul."

O God, our merciful Father, there is no sin that You exclude, but Your Son, our Savior, transmitted to His Church the power to forgive all sins without exception and without limitation. He said: "*Whatever* you loose on earth..." (Mt. 16:19; 18:18). *Whatever*—whether great or little.

Jesus extended this power, making it as general as possible, with the words, "those whose sins you forgive..." (Jn. 20:22).**

His words in Mark 3:28-29: "Truly, I say to you, all sins will be forgiven the sons of men, and whatever blasphemies they utter; but whoever blasphemes against the Holy Spirit never has forgiveness, but is guilty of an eternal sin" refer to the sins of perverse impenitents who stubbornly want to remain in their sins, and do not open themselves to Your Spirit of Love who inspires them to repent and be converted.

Your Son Himself had exercised this unlimited power by forgiving even the most grievous sins, such as those of the adulterous woman (cf. Jn. 7:53—8:11), the woman who was a public sinner (Lk. 7:36-50), the good thief (Lk. 23:43), and Peter himself and his denial (Lk. 22:61ff.).

Confidence in God

How wise is Your holy Church, O God, which revised the rite of Penance in order to exhort us to confidence in You, by reading in Your holy Bible Your teachings and examples of infinite mercy. No sinner should become discouraged, but feel confident that he will be welcomed by You, our heavenly Father, who gave Your Son to die for our sins.

The Fathers of the Church witness to the generality of the Church's power to forgive sins. In speaking about the sacrament of Penance, St. Ambrose says: "God makes no distinction; He promised His mercy to all, and has conferred the power of forgiveness on all His priests without exception."

Objectors say: "Why should we accuse ourselves of sin to a priest and not directly to God?" The answer is: Jesus Himself transferred the power to forgive sins to His Apostles and their legitimate successors. They forgive *in His name* and *with His authority*.

O God, You are the One whom we offend with our sins and, therefore, You should be the One to establish the conditions for forgiveness—not we, the offenders. In fact, because of our malice we should not even expect Your forgiveness. But since You are so merciful, we should at least accept the conditions You stated—to appreciate and receive the sacrament of Penance.

In our pride, we deal with You as we would with our neighbor. We want to discuss and dialogue. Yet even in our own day, there are still innumerable persons who are genuine followers of Christ, and they—adults and children alike—esteem this sacrament greatly.

Recently, in a sixth grade religion class two of the boys asked to be excused for a little while in order to go to confession. One said, "I did something very wrong. I really want to go to confession. I'll be back in a few minutes."

The words of Jesus "whose sins you forgive, they are forgiven" demand a juridical process which in this case means that the priest has to have knowledge of the state of the penitent (through the accusation) in order to pronounce the sentence (to absolve or withhold absolution).

In commenting on Matthew 18:18, St. John Chrysostom says: "The judge sits on earth; the Lord acts according to His servant, and whatever the latter judges on earth, that judgment is ratified in heaven."

At this point a question may be asked by delicate souls: "What about a priest who says to his penitent that some sins such as abortion, use of the pill, etc., are not sins?" The only answer we can give is that of St. Teresa of Avila: "Choose a confessor who is wise and holy."

"Let Your Hearts Be Broken...."

After a careful examination of conscience, and confession of sins, the imposition of a penance follows. This, together with the penitent's sorrow, confession of sins and resolution of amendment, are the conditions for good reception of the sacrament of Penance.

Sorrow does not consist in feelings, O God. So a penitent need not feel like a hypocrite if he has no *feeling* of repentance. Sorrow is not an emotion but an interior act of the understanding and will. The prophet Joel, speaking Your words to Your people, says:

"Let your hearts be broken, not your garments torn,
turn to Yahweh your God again,
for he is all tenderness and compassion,
slow to anger, rich in graciousness,
and ready to relent" (Joel 2:13).**

However, the sorrow should not be merely a natural one, such as: "I'm sorry because I have now lost my good reputation," or other similar motives. True sorrow must spring from a higher motive and be directed toward reconciliation with You and with Your people, O God, since in sinning we have offended both.

The highest degree of sorrow is *perfect* sorrow. It proceeds from the motive of perfect love of You—a love that begins with thankfulness, and appreciation for Your goodness shown in innumerable benefits, especially the greatest benefit, our redemption by the death of Jesus on the cross and His resurrection. Perfect love is the love of You, for Your own sake. It is the love of You for Yourself, because You are all good and deserving of all our love.

Imperfect sorrow is also a supernatural sorrow. It is based on the consideration of the wickedness of sin and/or the fear of hell and other punishments. That this sorrow is also pleasing to You, O God, is proved by Your warnings contained in the Holy Bible. In pointing out the divine punishment, Your Son says:

"Do not be afraid of those who kill the body but cannot kill the soul; fear him rather who can destroy both body and soul in hell" (Mt. 10:28).**

It is clear that sorrow should always be proved genuine by *the purpose of amendment*, that is, the resolve not to commit sin again. Jesus said to a man He had cured:

"Now you are well again, be sure not to sin any more, or something worse may happen to you" (Jn. 5:14).**

Who Should Go to Confession?

O God, Your holy Church has understood the importance of this sacrament so well that, always concerned for the salvation of her children, she has prescribed as a general Church law at least a yearly confession in case of serious sin (Fourth Lateran Council, 1215 A.D., and the Council of Trent). This is a duty not only for adults but begins with the years of discretion, that is, from the start of the use of reason at about the seventh year.

May You, O Lord, guide the hearts and wills of those who deny this sacrament of mercy and grace to Your little ones.

Your holy Pope, St. Pius X, had for children the heart of Your divine Son, and thus he decreed in his document *Quam singulari* (August 8, 1910) that children who have reached the age of discretion should receive the sacraments of Penance and the Eucharist. The application of this decree throughout the universal Church produced fruits in the Christian spiritual life.

On April 11, 1971, the *General Catechetical Directory* was promulgated. Pope John Paul II has said that "the *General Catechetical Directory* is still the basic document for encouraging and guiding catechetical renewal throughout the Church." In the Addendum of this document the custom of children receiving the sacrament of Penance before First Communion was confirmed (no. 5). The same document considered some new practices whereby admission to First Communion was authorized without previous confession. After two years of experimentation, the Sacred Congregations for the Discipline of the Sacraments and Divine Worship and for the Clergy, with the approval of Pope Paul VI, declared that these experiments were to cease at the end of the scholastic year 1972-73, and from that time on the Church was to observe the Decree *Quam singulari* of Saint Pius X.

It is not necessary to tell You, O Lord, that the reversal of what *Quam singulari* decreed was created by some opinions based on psychological and pedagogical arguments, the most prominent of which was the theory that young children are incapable of mortal sin. If it is true—and it is—that young children, before attaining the use of reason, are incapable of a personal sin, seven-

or eight-year-olds *are* capable of at least venial sin because everyone assumes this is the age of reason. In fact, it is at this age that they go to school.

Certainly, even a century ago St. Pius X had extensive knowledge of human nature, and thus decided on that age for children to receive both of these sacraments. Moreover, if children of a century ago could have used the sacrament of Penance, how much more Your little ones of today, who are exposed to the influence of TV, films, comic books and other printed matter, as well as bad example set by things done or said before them which they understand and keep in their minds or act upon.

Once again in May of 1977, the Church issued a document on *Confession and First Communion of Children.* Among other reasons supporting first confession before First Communion, it states that St. Paul's admonition truly establishes a directive norm which regards even children. The Apostle wrote: "Let a man examine himself, and so eat of the bread and drink of the cup" (1 Cor. 11:28).

Therefore, children also should examine themselves before receiving the Eucharist. "But often the child is not able to examine his conscience clearly and surely by himself," the document points out, and so he should be helped by a confessor or spiritual director. The children's parents too have a very important role to play, the document continues, in the spiritual formation of their children, and they have the right to be heard by those who educate their youngsters.

What a paradox, O Lord, that everyone—beginning with parents, teachers and ecclesiastical and civil authorities—wants an education for our children and youth which condemns vice and fosters virtue, yet, undoubtedly, the loss of innocence in many of the very young is due to this error of depriving children of the sacrament of Penance until a later age. And how very difficult it is then to bring them to the sacraments at all, because by that time they might have acquired bad habits which are in radical conflict with Your law, O God—a law which will be very hard for them to observe when they come to know it more fully. Therefore, postponing confession to a later age might easily increase rather than solve difficulties.

A priest sadly confided how he had participated in the experimentation of delaying first Penance in his parish. "We prepared the class of twenty for their First Communion, with the intention of having them make First Penance the next year. However, the following year only five came back to catechetical instruction classes. I often wonder about the other fifteen, whether they will ever make their first confession. I have been unsuccessful in contacting most of them, and in great part I feel responsible for their not having received this sacrament."

At the age of discretion a child in our day does know what is right or wrong. He should be treated as a "little man," rather than a "little tot." In fact, the above cited document adds, "If they can receive the Eucharist in a conscious way, suitable for their age, they can also have an equal awareness of sin and ask God's pardon in confession." Therefore, "it would be an absurd and unjust discrimination and a violation of [their] conscience if [they] were prepared for and admitted only to Holy Communion. It is not enough to say that children have the right to go to confession if this right remains practically ignored.

"When children are sufficiently instructed and are aware of the special nature of these two sacraments, it will not be difficult for them to go first to the sacrament of Reconciliation which—in a simple but fundamental way—arouses in them the awareness of moral good and evil and aids them to bring a more mature disposition to their happy meeting with Christ. The basic persuasion about the need of the greatest purity for receiving the Eucharist worthily, if prudently instilled in children right from the time of their First Communion, will accompany them for the rest of their lives and will lead to a greater esteem for, and a more frequent use of the sacrament of Reconciliation."

To conclude, O Lord, the most suitable age for children to receive the sacrament of Penance appears to be, for all the above-mentioned reasons, the age of seven to eight years, identified by St. Pius X. The child at this age, who is very sensitive to his love for You, will examine his conscience and feel sorry for whatever offense he has done to You or to his neighbor.

Moreover, the proper effect of the sacrament of Penance is not only the remission of sin but it is also freedom from a sense of guilt and is a source of joy, encouragement, strength against temptations, and spiritual growth.

56 THE SACRAMENTS AND YOU

During a catechetical meeting, one young woman asked to take the floor. The topic being discussed was the advantages of First Penance preceding First Communion.

"In our parish," she said, "Father trains the youngsters for first confession about a year before their First Communion. It is a beautiful sight to see the children conversing with the priest as a real spiritual father. He cares for each of them individually, and they sense this concern. They love Father and are anxious to go to confession even on a weekly basis."

Even though the faults of children of this age may be only trivial, they are *faults* nonetheless, which hinder the grace-filled soul from responding to Your Holy Spirit, O God.

How wise was Your servant, Cardinal Newman. While still an Anglican, he gave a sermon in which he warned that even slight or negligible sins may have devastating effects on one's moral character in Your sight, O Lord. He begins his reflections with citing the probable influence upon us of faults committed in our childhood, and even infancy, which we never realize or have altogether forgotten. The following are his words, as reported by the late John Cardinal Wright*:

"Ignorant as we may be when children begin to be responsible beings, yet we are ignorant also when they are not so; nor can we assign a date ever so early at which they certain-

---

First Confession and First Communion, available from the Daughters of St. Paul at any of the addresses at the end of this book. 36 pages, — PM0750

ly are not. And even the latest assignable date is very early; and thenceforward whatever they do exerts, we cannot doubt, a most momentous influence on their character. We know that two lines, starting at a small angle, diverge to greater and greater distances the further they are produced; and surely in like manner a soul living on into eternity may be infinitely changed for the better or the worse by very slight influences exerted on it in the beginning of its course. A very slight deviation at setting out may be the measure of the difference between tending to hell and tending to heaven."

God Is Eager To Forgive and So Is His Church

If sinners only knew how eager You are to forgive them, O Father, they would follow the example of the prodigal son, who after a life of sin concluded: "I will...go to my father and say: Father, I have sinned against heaven and against you..." (Lk. 15:18).**

There is no reason to worry about exposing one's sins in a *secret* confession. We read in history of priests who were martyred for keeping this secret. An outstanding example is St. John Nepomucene, who refused to tell the King the sins of his wife, the Queen. The priest was thrown into a river and drowned at the command of the King.

There are two kinds of sins. One, a *deadly* sin, deprives the soul of true life or "eternal life," and is also called *grave* or *mortal* sin. Such a sin is committed when a person *knowingly* and *willfully* does anything which is seriously against the law of God. If unforgiven, mortal sin leads to eternal punishment.

Mortal sins are all to be confessed, according to their kind, number and those circumstances which alter their nature (cf. Post-Synodal Apostolic Exhortation on Reconciliation and Penance, Pope John Paul II). Thus, if after a careful examination of conscience one should *knowingly* omit confessing only one mortal sin, he would render the sacrament invalid, and none of his sins would be forgiven. Instead, he would add a new and greater sin—a sacrilege.

St. John Chrysostom wrote: "The devil makes people bold in committing sins. Afterwards, however, he makes them feel ashamed of confessing them."

St. Teresa of Avila gave this advice to the Carmelite Fathers: "Preach often against sacrilegious confessions because God revealed to me that the majority of Christians go to hell because of incomplete confessions."

St. Augustine stated: "You will be damned if you withhold; while you could free yourself if you would confess."

St. Charles Borromeo said: "Most of the time the penitents go to confession more as a habit, than out of knowing their sins with a will to correct themselves."

Should one, however, after a diligent examination of conscience, *forget* a mortal sin, his/her confession is valid, and even the forgotten sin is remitted with the others. The person, therefore, can receive Communion, but he/she has to confess that sin in the next confession.

In the life of the holy Curé of Ars, written by P. Manin, it is recorded that "the greater number of those who came to Ars would make a general confession. The saint was always at their disposition, knowing that this (confession) was the means of preventing many souls from going to hell, since with their general confessions they made reparation for their sacrilegious confessions."

O God, may Your holy Mother, Refuge of sinners, obtain from Jesus the grace that both in life and at death, all will confess their sins with sincerity and sorrow.

Frequent Confession

When sins are of the other type, *venial*—venial sins are less serious offenses against God's law—it is not obligatory to confess them since they are not deadly, that is, they do not remove Your life or sanctifying grace from our souls. They can be expiated by many other means, such as sorrow, prayer, works of charity, reception of Holy Communion, Holy Mass, etc. However, it is permissible, good and profitable to confess them too, as Your Church teaches.

In fact, in his encyclicals *Mystici Corporis* and *Mediator Dei*, Pius XII recommended the frequent reception of the sacrament of Penance, calling it "the pious practice of frequent confession, introduced by the Church under the guidance of the Holy Spirit."

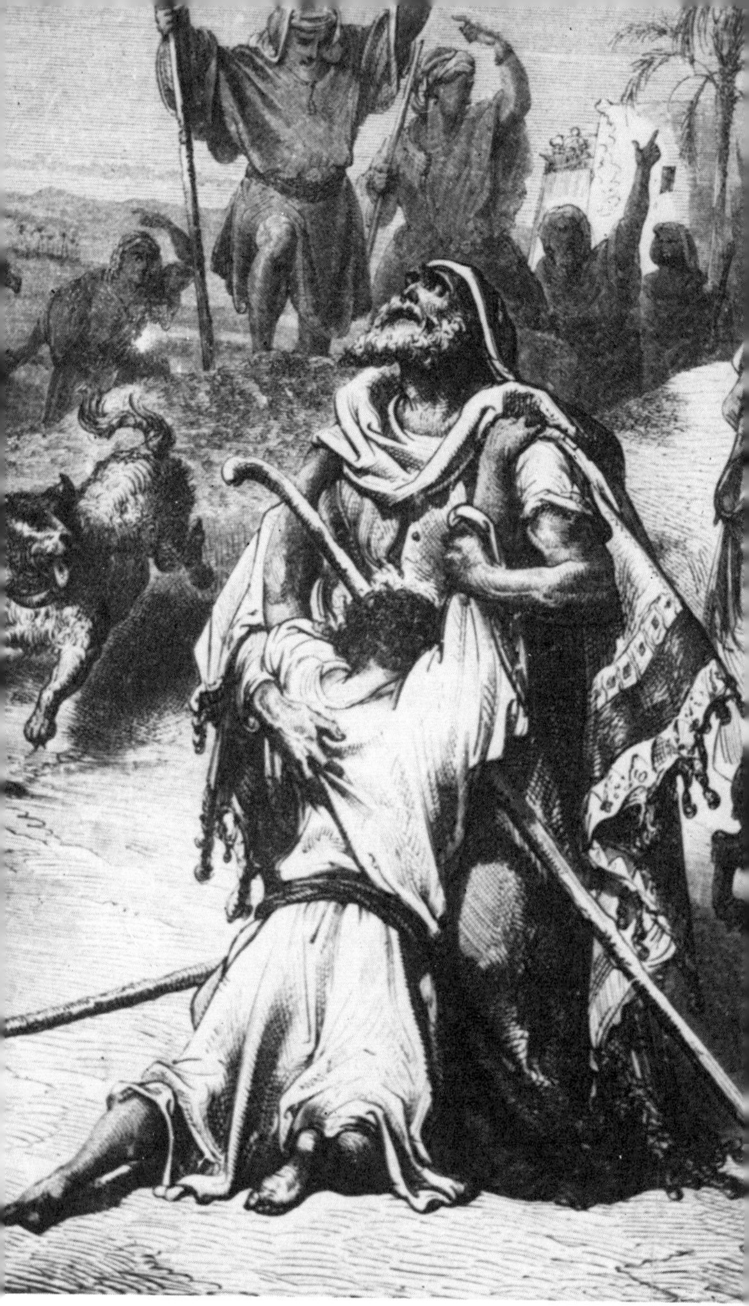

Venial sins weaken one's resistance to serious sin, and make the sinner deserving of temporal punishment. Thus, in her post-conciliar document, *Pastoral Norms Concerning the Administration of General Sacramental Absolution*, which is issued by Your Church, O God, there is a most important point, in which priests are exhorted in this regard. We would like to quote it here:

"Priests should be careful not to discourage the faithful from frequent or devotional confession. On the contrary, let them draw attention to its fruitfulness for Christian living (cf. *Mystici Corporis*, A.A.S. 35 [1943], 235) and always display readiness to hear such a confession whenever a reasonable request is made by the faithful. It must be absolutely prevented that individual confession should be reserved for serious sins only, for this would deprive the faithful of the great benefit of confession and would injure the good name of those who approach the sacrament singly" (no. 12).

Pope John Paul II adds: "It is the right of each penitent; and one can even say that it is the right of Christ, with regard to each person whom He has redeemed, to be able to say through His minister: 'Your sins are forgiven' " (cf. *Redemptor hominis*, no. 20).

Celebrate Penance

Beautiful, O Lord, are the so-called "liturgical celebrations and community rites of Penance." They have great usefulness for the preparation of a more fruitful confession of sins and amendment of life. They are composed of various parts: *opening prayers; reading of the Bible*, preferably from the Gospel, which is the Good News of salvation; *an examination of conscience; an expression of sorrow; individual confession* and *absolution; proclamation of praise* to You, all-merciful God; and *a concluding prayer of thanksgiving.*

These celebrations are not at all to be confused with the third form of reconciliation permitted in cases of danger of death. In this case, after a brief instruction, the priest invites the faithful who wish to receive general absolution to repent of their sins, resolve not to sin again, to make up for any scandal or harm they may have caused, and to confess *individually* at the proper time each of the serious sins which they cannot now confess. He will also add some form of penance for all.

This same rite of reconciliation of several penitents with general confession and absolution is permitted also when there is a serious necessity, with the authorization of the bishop, namely, in the words of the Church, "when in view of the number of penitents there are not enough confessors at hand to hear properly the confessions of each within an appropriate time, with the result that the penitents through no fault of their own would be forced to do without sacramental grace or Holy Communion for a long time. This can happen especially in mission lands but also in and within groups where it is clear that this need exists.

"This is not lawful, however, when confessors are able to be at hand, merely because of a great concourse of penitents such as can for example occur on a great feast or pilgrimage" (no. 3).

In this last case, the rite takes place as described above. The new revised rite stresses that a person who receives general absolution from grave sins is bound to confess each grave sin at his next individual confession. And in the words of the Document *Pastoral Norms Concerning the Administration of General Sacramental Absolution:* "They are strictly obliged, unless prevented by moral impossibility, to go to confession within a year," because "they too are affected by the precept that obliges every Christian to confess privately to a priest once a year at least all his serious sins that he has not yet specifically confessed" (no. 7).*

To Grow in Grace

A word yet, O Lord, on the way to confess. The words of Paul VI to a general audience, on April 3, 1974, are very helpful:

"You will also hear clarifications and rectifications of certain wrong information that has spread about the new rite of the sacrament of Penance, such as the abolition of confessionals. The confessional, as a protective screen between

---

* In addition to this obligation, Canon 963 of the New Code says that one whose grave sins were forgiven by a general absolution, is, as soon as possible, when the opportunity occurs, to make an individual confession before receiving another general absolution, unless a just reason intervenes.

the minister and the penitent, to guarantee the absolute secrecy of the conversation imposed on them and reserved for them, must, it is clear, remain. (We recall, for example, what Guitton writes about an extraordinary priest, a spiritual master, a very fine thinker, Father Guillaume Pouget, Lazzarist, who was often visited by all kinds of persons, often famous and important; they would go to his room and often they ended up by making their confession, because he was blind.)"

Your mercy, O God the Father of mercies, is infinite. You do not wish the sinner to die but to turn back to You and live. You gave us every means to absolve us from our sins, to cleanse our souls and clothe us with Your grace, which also brings peace of mind and heart.

Your sacrament of Reconciliation or Penance is necessary for salvation to those who after Baptism fall into grievous sin. The very purpose of this sacrament is the reconciling of sinners with You, and some of the effects of Penance are: the remission of mortal sin, the reconciliation of the sinner with You by the infusion of sanctifying grace, the remission of the eternal punishment and at least some of the temporal punishment due to our sins, and the revival of the merits due to good works performed in the state of grace, which were rendered null by grievous sin.

The reception of this sacrament by baptized persons who have only venial sins to confess or sins of the past life already confessed, is a most useful means to correct defects and to grow in Your grace and in virtue.

Persons who want to really make progress in the spiritual life are unanimously advised by spiritual directors and confessors to approach this sacrament frequently because it helps prevent serious falls. In addition, the sacrament of Penance gives the soul a kind of right with You, O God, to actual graces and a special strength to avoid even small faults.

There were saints in the past and there are saints living today who have used and use this sacrament twice a week and even every day. Those who receive the sacrament of Penance for the remission of venial sins are more certain of their forgiveness because among all the means for the remission of venial sins, this sacrament is the most efficacious, since this is its very purpose, as instituted by Jesus Christ for the remission of sins.

Moreover, every time one receives this sacrament of forgiveness, one also receives an increase of sanctifying grace, of sanctity, with the right to a greater glory in heaven.

There are yet more good effects. The more one humiliates himself and detests his fault, the more temporal punishment is remitted. These persons build up a delicate conscience, diligent and vigilant, in order to avoid even every voluntary imperfection.

An act of *perfect* contrition, of course, restores sanctifying grace in us after grave sin, though we still should confess those grave sins.

The Sacrament of the Holy Eucharist

The Eucharist as a Sacrament

In our times, dear Lord, there is often tragic doubt about the greatest and holiest sacrament, the Eucharist. Too many today doubt the Real Presence of Your Son in this sacrament of love.

Recently, a well-intentioned college student was questioning his bishop about certain truths of the Faith. At one point the bishop asked, "What do you think of the Eucharist?"

"What do you mean?" the young man replied.

"Do you believe that Jesus is *really* present in the Holy Eucharist or that His is a symbolic presence?"

The young man quickly answered, "I go to Mass and Communion faithfully, but I certainly don't believe that Christ is actually there. I believe the sacrament is a symbol of His presence."

The fatherly bishop, knowing the sincerity of the young man, asked further: "Do you believe in the Bible?"

"Certainly I do. It's God's word," said the student.

Then the bishop proceeded, "Let's open St. John's Gospel to chapter six and read the discourse of Jesus on the Eucharist." And he began quoting some passages:

" 'I am the bread of life.... I am the living bread which came down from heaven; if anyone eats of this bread, he will live forever; and the bread which I shall give for the life of the world is my flesh.... My flesh is food indeed, and my blood is drink indeed. He who eats my flesh and drinks my blood abides in me, and I in him.' "

With what impact did these unmistakable words strike the young man. Open to grace, he said, "It's so clear. I wonder why I never understood them like I do now." Then and there, without any further explanation, he believed in the Real Presence of Your Son in the Holy Eucharist!

The unfortunate denial today of the Real Presence of Christ in the Holy Eucharist is nothing but a repetition of the error of Berengarius of Tours in the Middle Ages and later of the Reformers. If people knew history and the proofs given in the past by Your Church, they would not be influenced by errors such as these: "Bread and wine are mere *symbols* or *figures* of the body and blood of Christ." "The Mass is only a meal."

What is most disturbing is the fact that this unbelief leads to disrespect in words and deeds for the Blessed Sacrament.

How far are these people from the truth, Lord, and consequently from the precious effects brought about by faith and good dispositions in participating in the Mass and receiving Communion.

Body and Blood of Christ

In the Mass or Eucharistic Celebration, when the words of Consecration have been pronounced, the reality of bread and wine is totally changed into the body and blood of Christ, and this wonderful change is called *transubstantiation*.

The Eucharist is the sacrament instituted by Your Son at the Last Supper and it is both a sacrament and a sacrifice. In this sacrament Christ Your Son, under the appearances of bread and wine, is truly present, as true God and true man, in body, blood, soul and divinity, in order to offer Himself in an unbloody manner to You, heavenly Father, and to give Himself to us as nourishment for our souls.

Already in the Old Testament we find the Eucharist prefigured: the tree of life in paradise; the sacrifices of Abraham and Melchizedek; the manna in the desert; the various sacrifices of the Old Testament, especially that of the Paschal Lamb.

In the New Testament Jesus promised the Holy Eucharist. His words were most clear in the Gospel of St. John:

"I am the living bread which came down from heaven; if any one eats of this bread, he will live for ever; and the bread which I shall give for the life of the world is my flesh" (6:51).

The Jews had understood, and they disputed among themselves, "How can this man give us his flesh to eat?" (6:52) At this, Jesus did not retract what He had said, but confirmed it:

"Truly, truly, I say to you, unless you eat the flesh of the Son of man and drink his blood, you have no life in you; he who eats my flesh and drinks my blood has eternal life, and I will raise him up at the last day" (6:53-54).

Many of His disciples left Jesus at this point, but He did not alter one word of what He had said. He wanted His words to have a literal interpretation.

Then, turning to His Twelve, Jesus said, "Will you also go away?" (6:67) But Simon Peter answered Him, as You enlightened him, O Father: "Lord, to whom shall we go? You have the words of eternal life; and we have believed, and have come to know, that you are the Holy One of God" (6:68-69).

Faith is Your gift, O God. As in all the mysteries of our Faith we believe in the Real Presence of Jesus in the Holy Eucharist because Your Son is God like You, and with His almighty power He is able to perform this great miracle. By it He remains with us to nourish our souls with Himself—the Bread of Life—so that, filled with love for You and our neighbor, we may become more and more a people acceptable to You.

We read in Your Bible not only of the promise of the Eucharist, but also and repeatedly of the fulfillment, that is, about the institution of this most sublime sacrament.

In the Gospel of St. Matthew we read:

"Now as they were eating, Jesus took bread, and blessed, and broke it, and gave it to the disciples and said, 'Take, eat; **this is my body.**' And he took a cup, and when he had given thanks he gave it to them, saying, 'Drink of it, all of you; for **this is my blood** of the covenant, which is poured out for many for the forgiveness of sins' " (26:26-28).

In the Gospel of St. Mark we read:

"And as they were eating, he took bread, and blessed, and broke it, and gave it to them, and said, 'Take; **this is my body.**' And he took a cup, and when he had given thanks he gave it to them, and they all drank of it. And he said to them, '**This is my blood** of the covenant, which is poured out for many. Truly, I say to you, I shall not drink again of the fruit of the vine until that day when I drink it new in the kingdom of God' " (14:22-25).

In the Gospel of St. Luke we read:

"And he said to them, 'I have earnestly desired to eat this passover with you before I suffer; for I tell you I shall not eat it until it is fulfilled in the kingdom of God.' And he took a cup, and when he had given thanks he said, 'Take this, and divide it among yourselves; for I tell you that from now on I shall not drink of the fruit of the vine until the kingdom of God comes.' And he took bread, and when he had given thanks he broke it and gave it to them, saying, '**This is my body** which is given for you. Do this in remembrance of me.' And likewise the cup after supper, saying, '**This** cup which is poured out for you **is the new covenant in my blood**' " (22:15-20).

St. Paul, also, to whom You revealed Yourself, wrote in his first epistle to the Corinthians:

"For I received from the Lord what I also delivered to you, that the Lord Jesus on the night when he was betrayed took bread, and when he had given thanks, he broke it, and said, '**This is my body** which is for you. Do this in remembrance of me.' In the same way also the cup, after supper, saying, '**This cup is the new covenant in my blood.** Do this, as often as you drink it, in remembrance of me' " (1 Cor. 11:23-25).

In the same letter, St. Paul also refers to the unworthy reception of the Eucharist, and he sees in this nothing less than sinning against the body and blood of the Lord, a sin which is worthy of condemnation:

"Whoever, therefore, eats the bread or drinks the cup of the Lord in an unworthy manner will be guilty of profaning the body and blood of the Lord. Let a man examine himself, and so eat of the bread and drink of the cup. For any one who eats and drinks without discerning the body eats and drinks judgment upon himself" (1 Cor. 11:27-29).

Just as explicit is the following reflection of the great Apostle:

"The cup of blessing which we bless, is it not a participation in the blood of Christ? The bread which we break, is it not a participation in the body of Christ?" (1 Cor. 10:16)

I recall, O God, the story of a non-Catholic university student who was reading a Catholic Bible. When she came upon the same passages referred to above, You touched her mind and heart through Your Holy Spirit, and she believed. She immediately confronted these passages with her own Bible, and upon finding them the same, she asked herself, "Why, O Lord, didn't I believe in Your Real Presence before now?"

You never deny the grace of faith to those who ask it of You with humility and confidence.

Faith of the Early Church

The Fathers of the Church, too, reflected the belief of the first Christians in the Real Presence.

St. Ignatius of Antioch, speaking about the heretical Docetists of his time, says: "They keep away from the Eucharist because they do not confess that the Eucharist is the flesh of our Redeemer, Jesus Christ...."

St. Justin Martyr describes in his First Apologia the primitive Christian Eucharistic celebration, and he says of the Eucharistic banquet: "We receive this not as ordinary bread and ordinary drink"; but as "both flesh and blood of that same incarnate Jesus."

St. Irenaeus of Lyons attests: "The bread over which thanksgiving is pronounced, is the body of the Lord and the chalice of His blood."

Tertullian expresses his faith in the Real Presence thus: "The flesh is refreshed with the body and blood of Christ so that the soul also may be nourished by God."

St. Augustine professes this belief in the Real Presence in association with the words of the institution: "The bread which you see on the altar is, sanctified by the word of God, the body of Christ; that chalice, or rather what is contained in the chalice, is, sanctified by the word of God, the blood of Christ." He also writes in reference to the institution of the Eucharist at the Last Supper: "Christ bore Himself in His hands, when He offered His body, saying: 'This is my body.' "

Yes, Lord, as St. Augustine says, it is in the Mass or Eucharistic Celebration, when the priest speaks the words Your Son used in instituting this sacrament, that he speaks them in the Person of Christ, and he effects this sacrament. Therefore, "immediately after the Consecration," as the Council of Trent teaches, that is, after the uttering of the words of institution, the true body and the true blood of the Lord are present on the altar.

This transformation of the whole substance of the bread into the body of Christ and the whole substance of the wine into the blood of Christ is possible only to Your Son, who is almighty God, capable of doing all things. It is not difficult for people of faith to believe with the same faith of our fathers, since our Faith is unchangeable throughout the centuries. The expression of St. Cyril of Jerusalem is in place here: "Once at Cana in Galilee, by a mere nod, Christ changed water into wine, and is it now incredible that He changes wine into blood?"

Because of the mandate Your Son gave to His Apostles right after the institution: "Do this in remembrance of me" (Lk. 22:19), and because of the power You gave to Your priests in the sacrament of Holy Orders, only a validly ordained priest truly effects this wondrous sacrament.

How thankful we are, O God, for Your having given us our Redeemer who died, rose, ascended into heaven, where He sits at Your right hand, and yet really remains in our midst in the Blessed Sacrament!

What Kind of Bread and Wine?

Lord, permit me another digression. This time it concerns abuses taking place in our day as regards valid matter—bread and wine—to be used for Mass.

The words of a bishop, spoken lately to the clergy, religious and laity of his diocese, are an important message for all of us at this time in the Church. He writes:

"My brothers and sisters in Christ:

"Over the past several months, some inquiries have been received about valid and licit matter for the Holy Eucharist. On occasion I have found myself wondering about the appropriateness of certain types of bread and wine which were presented for consecration during the Masses I have celebrated. I write to offer some clarifications on the subject.

"The years since the Second Vatican Council have seen quite a bit of experimentation with the proper bread for the Eucharist. This was basically in response to the General Instruction of the Roman Missal which, in addition to reaffirming the tradition of the Latin Church that the bread must be made from wheat and be unleavened (no. 282), also stated that the 'nature of the sign demands that the material for the eucharistic celebration appear as actual food...' (no. 283).

"The Congregation for the Doctrine of the Faith some months ago conveyed to the bishops of the United States a reminder in this matter. The congregation, with the approval of the Holy

Father, emphasized that the only acceptable ingredients for the Mass breads are pure wheaten flour and water. If slight additions of other ingredients are made, then the bread becomes illicit material for the Eucharist. If there is a substitution of all or of a large quantity of the water by other liquids (e.g. by milk, honey, eggs, etc.), the resultant product is, in the judgment of the Congregation, invalid matter for the Eucharist. In other words, bread for use in the Mass must be made solely of wheaten flour and water, nothing else whatsoever may be used.

"The Holy See thus makes clear that we must interpret the Instruction of the Roman Missal (no. 283) as employing only the elements of flour and water. Some have sought to use a kind of bread more closely resembling that of our daily use. Various recipes have been employed which while not using yeast (leaven) yet result in a product more like our cake.

"I do not minimize the sincerity and conviction of those who seek to offer a kind of bread more readily perceived as food by the people of our time and culture. Yet we must remember that even the austere unleavened bread of the Roman Rite is made of true wheaten flour and is of itself a physically nourishing substance that can indeed serve as an authentic symbol in our sharing of the heavenly Food of the Eucharist.

"To stress this symbol of actual food I strongly recommend to our parishes that, whenever possible, the hosts be somewhat larger in size and of greater thickness than in the past. Indeed, no. 283 of the General Instruction encourages this more authentic sign so that the one bread, blessed and broken, may be shared among many—as was the original practice of the Church. Since the priest is urged to consecrate breads for Communion at every celebration of the Mass, there should be less pressure to reserve large quantities of hosts in the tabernacle. It was that need in the past which often led to the use of paper-thin hosts less suited as Eucharistic signs. The recent extension of the permission to distribute Communion under both kinds brings out the same point: the authenticity of the signs used in our sacramental celebrations.

"As for the wine employed for the Eucharist, it must be the fermented juice of the grape. Wine produced from other substances is clearly improper and invalid material for the Mass. And since even grape wine can be manipulated and altered chemically in so many ways, it is important that only those grape wines be used which have received explicit approval for Catholic sacramental purposes.

"I ask your complete cooperation in this serious matter. It is important that we be most careful in all that treats the elements of the Eucharist; in these matters we must follow carefully the directives of the Holy See. We do not have the option of employing materials which can raise questions, evoke scruples or encourage impropriety. These are alien to the Eucharistic celebration.

"May the Lord Jesus, truly and substantially present in the Sacrament of the Altar, bless us all in our fidelity to His Word and to His Church."

Sincerely in Christ,
(Most Rev.) James A. Hickey
Bishop of Cleveland*

Yes, O God almighty, we believe that the body and the blood of Christ, together with His soul and His divinity, and therefore the whole Christ, are truly present in the Eucharist. We believe that because Christ is risen, He is totally present under each of the two species, that is, totally present under the appearance of bread and totally present under the appearance of wine.

We believe that worship or adoration must be given to our Lord Jesus Christ, present in the Holy Eucharist. Your faithful believers, in fact, bow down in adoration and make an act of faith by answering, "Amen" (I believe) when the priest says, "The body of Christ" to each person while giving Communion. Even the first Christians did the same, as St. Augustine wrote: "Nobody eats this flesh without previously adoring It."

Our Meeting With Christ

In referring to the habit of many today, who seem to receive Communion without previ-

---

* Reprinted with the gracious permission of His Excellency. Most Rev. James A. Hickey is now the Archbishop of Washington.

ous preparation, John Paul II, in the letter he addressed to all the bishops of the Church, *Dominicae cenae*, writes:

"When we realize who it is that we receive in Eucharistic Communion, there springs up in us almost spontaneously a sense of unworthiness, together with sorrow for our sins and an interior need for purification.

"But we must always take care that this great meeting with Christ in the Eucharist does not become a mere habit, and that we do not receive Him unworthily, that is to say, in a state of mortal sin....

"Sometimes, indeed quite frequently, everybody participating in the eucharistic assembly goes to Communion; and on some such occasions, as experienced pastors confirm, there has not been due care to approach the sacrament of Penance so as to purify one's conscience. This can of course mean that those approaching the Lord's table find nothing on their conscience, according to the objective law of God, to keep them from this sublime and joyful act of being sacramentally united with Christ. But there can also be, at least at times, another idea behind this: the idea of the Mass as *only* a banquet in which one shares by receiving the body of Christ in order to manifest, above all else, fraternal communion. It is not hard to add to these reasons a certain human respect and mere 'conformity'.... St. Paul's words, 'Let a man examine himself' (1 Cor. 11:28), are well known; this judgment is an indispensable condition for a personal decision whether to approach Eucharistic Communion or to abstain" (nos. 7, 11).

Certainly, there is no need for comment.

Communion in the Hand

Another important subject treated by the Pope in the same letter concerns the practice of receiving Communion in the hand. It is not only sad but horrifying to hear of how much disrespect is shown to Your divine Son by all too many people, both young and old. The Pope writes thus:

"This practice (of receiving Communion in the hand) has been requested by individual episcopal conferences and has received approval from the Apostolic See. However, cases of a deplorable lack of respect towards the eucharistic species have been reported, cases which are imputable not only to the individuals guilty of such behavior but also to the pastors of the Church who have not been vigilant enough regarding the attitude of the faithful towards the Eucharist. It also happens, on occasion, that the free choice of those who prefer to continue the practice of receiving the Eucharist on the tongue is not taken into account in those places where the distribution of Communion in the hand has been authorized. It is therefore difficult in the context of this present letter not to mention the sad phenomena previously referred to. This is in no way meant to refer to those who, receiving the Lord Jesus in the hand, do so with profound reverence and devotion, in those countries where this practice has been authorized" (no. 11).

THE SACRAMENT OF THE HOLY EUCHARIST 81

At this point, it seems opportune, O God, to repeat here with illustrations the instructions given by the United States Episcopal Conference for a respectful and devout reception of Communion in the hand.

*HOW TO RECEIVE
COMMUNION IN THE HAND:*

1. Place one hand on top of the other.

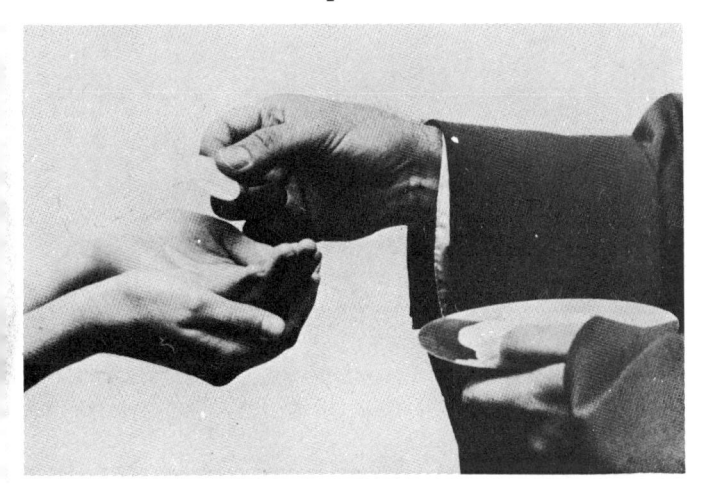

82 THE SACRAMENTS AND YOU

2. The priest says, "The body of Christ."
   You reply, "Amen."
   The Host is placed in your open hand.

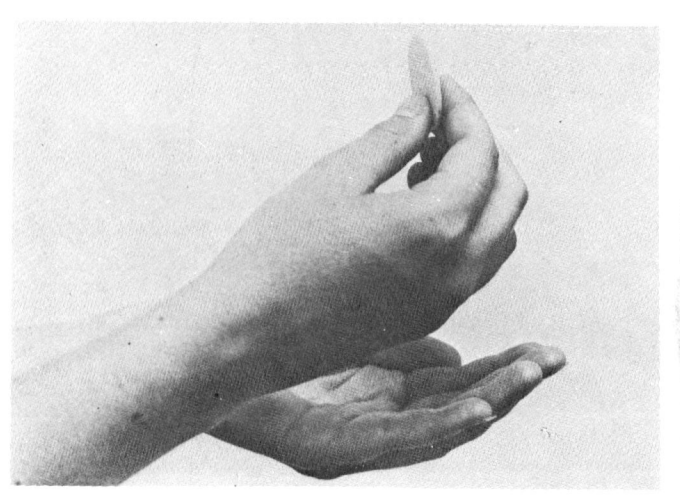

3. Take one step to the side, and then take the Host with your own hand.

4. Place the Host reverently into your mouth and then return to your place.

"I Will Give You Rest"

What a sublime gift Your Son gave to us, O God, in making it possible to receive Him in Eucharistic Communion. Only He who is God was capable of showing His love for us to the point of remaining with us in this most holy sacrament. He has said: "Come to me, all who labor and are heavy laden, and I will give you rest" (Mt. 11:28).

How much wiser would be those who have the difficult role of guidance, if they reminded those whom they counsel of these words of Your

Son. He is the Truth, and for those who believe, and receive Him in this sacrament, He brings about that peace of mind and soul which only You, O God, can give, together with many other divine effects. The chief of these are:

—Inner and physical union with Christ, who in this sacrament is physically present. He said, "He who eats my flesh and drinks my blood abides in me, and I in him" (Jn. 6:57).

From this union with Christ, the Head of the Mystical Body, flows the unity of the faithful with one another, because they are members of the Mystical Body. St. Paul says, "...we who are many are one body, for we all partake of the one bread" (1 Cor. 10:17). How important this is, O Father, since the virtue that Your Son recommended the most is love: "By this all men will know that you are my disciples, if you have love for one another" (Jn. 13:35).

Thus, the Fathers of the Church by preference stress this fruit of Holy Communion and call it "a sign of unity, a bond of charity."

—The Holy Eucharist also preserves and increases Your divine life in us; weakens evil concupiscence and reinforces the power of the will in overcoming temptations. Moreover, together with the increase of the life of grace, the virtues of faith, hope and charity, as well as the gifts of the Holy Spirit, are also associated.

—The Eucharist purifies our souls of venial sins and temporal punishment due to them. However, this last fruit is proportioned to the intensity of our love, which in practice is shown by a good preparation and thanksgiving.

—Holy Communion even brings about a spiritual joy, together with a joyful and peaceful acceptance of the duties and sacrifices of life. Here we could recall the words of St. Paul: "I rejoice in my sufferings" (Col. 1:24).

—Above all, the Eucharist is a pledge of our future glory and eternal happiness, as Jesus Himself said when He promised It: "He who eats my flesh and drinks my blood has eternal life, and I will raise him up at the last day" (Jn. 6:54). Concerning this marvelous effect, St. Irenaeus argues against the heretical Gnostics: "When our bodies partake of the Eucharist, they are no longer corruptible, because they have the hope of eternal resurrection."

After these reflections, O God, who wants to limit himself to receiving Jesus Christ in the Eucharist only once a year at Easter time? And how can a person who neglects for a notable period of time the reception of the Savior in the Eucharist be able to preserve the state of grace for a long time?

May Our Adoration Never Cease

After Vatican II, the custom of receiving Communion under both species was reintroduced. This beautiful and meaningful practice had been used in early Christian times, but was abolished in the Middle Ages for practical reasons, particularly because of the danger of profanation of the sacrament. Even today, O God, this danger is present and there are those who forget that Jesus is present in each and every part of the Host and in each and every drop of the blood, and they certainly should be much more reverent in receiving Him.

Out of reverence for the most holy sacrament and in order to prevent abuse, as St. Paul noted among the first Christians—"For in eating, each one goes ahead with his own meal, and one is hungry and another is drunk" (1 Cor. 11:21)—Your Church has from the fourth century demanded a fast as a bodily preparation for the worthy reception of the Eucharist. Notable changes in this law have been introduced in recent times, in view of the difficulties existing in many regions. The Church now requires a fast of one hour from all solid foods and liquids (both alcoholic and non-alcoholic), with the exception of water, which can be taken at any time, and medicine.

The sick and the elderly, as well as those who care for them, may receive even if within the preceding hour they have consumed something.

There are other minor objections to new concessions, for example, some devout persons, O Lord, feel that they should receive Holy Communion only in a kneeling position. They even make of it a problem of conscience. O Lord, do not let these good people be disturbed by such a simple matter. We know that even though kneeling is a sign of adoration, we are also aware that standing is a sign of respect. Your Church permits either position. Let them willingly adopt the method indicated by their pastors, as the Church teaches, "so that Communion may truly be a sign of brotherly union of all those who share in the same table of the Lord" *(Eucharisticum mysterium,* no. 34).

We believe, O God, that after the Consecration of the Mass—and more precisely, even after the Mass is over—the whole Christ is present in the Eucharist.

"Adoration of Christ in this sacrament of love," writes John Paul II in his letter "On the Mystery and Worship of the Eucharist" *(Dominicae cenae),* "must also find expression *in various forms of Eucharistic devotion;* personal prayer before the Blessed Sacrament, Hours of Adoration, periods of exposition—short, prolonged and annual (Forty Hours)—Eucharistic benediction, Eucharistic processions, Eucharistic congresses.... The Church and the world have a great need of Eucharistic worship. Jesus waits for us in this sacrament of love. Let us be generous with our time in going to meet Him in adoration and in contemplation that is full of faith and ready to make reparation for the great faults and crimes of the world. May our adoration never cease" (no. 3).

The Eucharist as a Sacrifice

After Vatican II, the expression "the Mass is a banquet" has become very popular. Certain types of non-liturgical music, dancing, hand-clapping and displays of affection have resulted, giving the impression that the Mass is nothing more than a social gathering, a mere banquet. However, Lord, Your Church has not changed her teaching in post-conciliar times. The Church defines that the Mass or Eucharistic Sacrifice is, first of all, a *sacrifice.* John Paul II in *Dominicae cenae* says, "The Eucharist is above all else a sacrifice. It is the sacrifice of the Redemption and also the sacrifice of the new covenant" (no. 9).

The Reformers rejected the sacrificial character of the Eucharist, or else accepted it only as a sacrifice in an imperfect sense. Their error proceeds from a wrong interpretation of the sacrifice of the Mass. Contrary to the Catholic Faith, which teaches that the Mass is *the renewal of the sacrifice of the cross,* the Reformers held that Catholics considered it as an independent sacrifice, side by side with the sacrifice of the cross. To make matters clear, O God, we are to establish here the difference between the *sacrament* of the Eucharist and the *sacrifice* of the Eucharist.

Although both are performed by the same Consecration, still they are distinct. In fact, the Eucharist is a sacrament insofar as in it Christ gives Himself as nourishment to our souls. It is a sacrifice insofar as in it Christ is offered to You, O God our Father, as a sacrificial gift.

As a sacrament, the Eucharist is the font of life by which we are cleansed, strengthened and sanctified. As a sacrifice, the Eucharist has the purpose of glorifying You, O God, and in it we offer ourselves to You with Christ, through Christ, and in Christ, for our own salvation and for that of the whole world.

We believe that in the sacrifice of the Mass Jesus Christ is present in His Word, and it is He Himself who speaks when the Holy Scriptures are read.

We believe that He is present when, after the Liturgy of the Word, the faithful unite their spiritual sacrifices, represented by the bread and wine, offer themselves as "a living sacrifice, holy and acceptable to God" (Rom. 12:1), in perfect union with His sacrifice.

We believe He is present when the faithful pray and sing for He promised: "For where two or three are gathered in my name, there am I in the midst of them" (Mt. 18:20).

We believe, O God, that the sacrifice of the Mass is the same sacrifice of the cross which Your Son Jesus Christ, our only Mediator with You, once offered on Calvary and now re-enacts on our altars for the forgiveness of those sins which we daily commit.

We believe that the Mass or Eucharistic sacrifice is the unbloody representation of the sacrifice of the cross for the application of Christ's saving power to us.

We believe that in the sacrifice of the Mass, our Lord Jesus Christ is immolated when, through the words of the Consecration, He becomes present on the altar under the appearances of bread and wine.

We believe that His presence is real, substantial, that is, He, the God-man, is wholly and entirely present on the altar after the Consecration. We cannot express in words this mode of

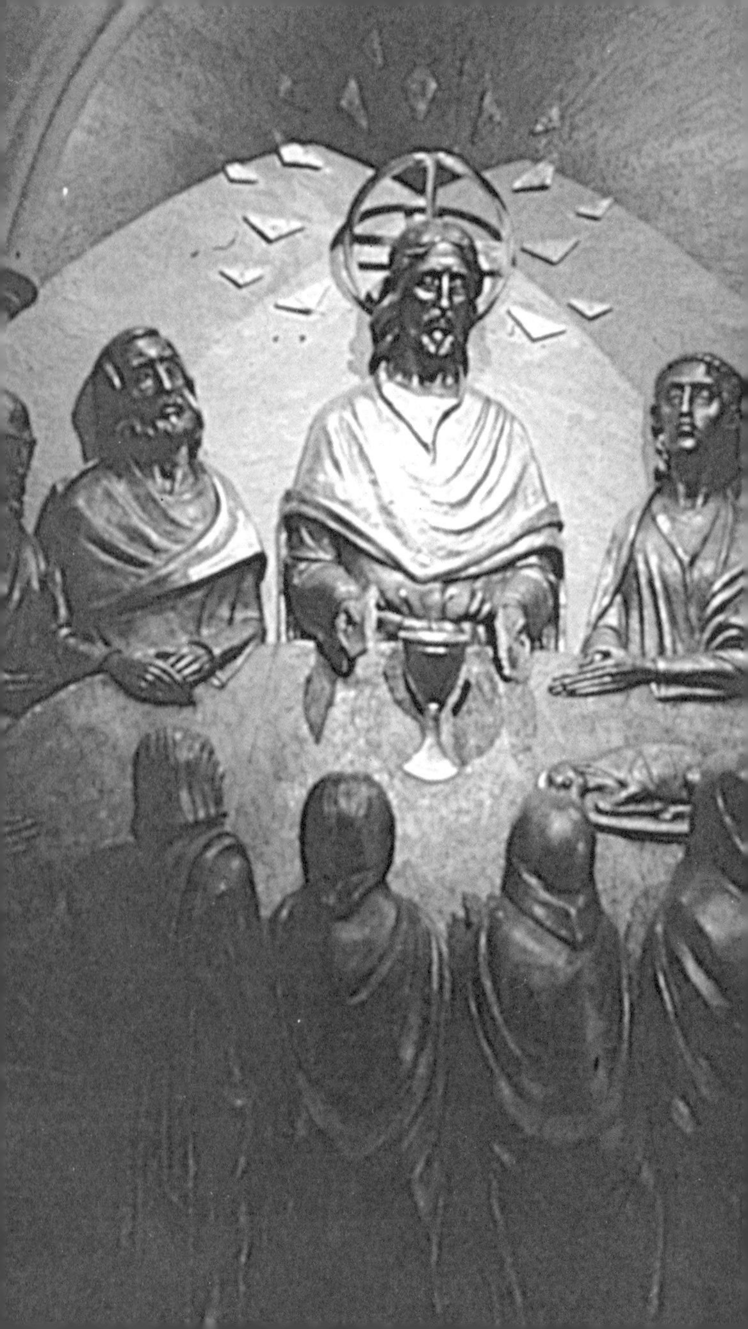

existence, but we believe, with a mind illumined by faith, that this great Mystery is possible to You, almighty God.

We believe that this unique and truly wonderful change of the whole substance of the bread into Christ's body and the whole substance of the wine into Christ's blood, is rightly called transubstantiation.

We believe that after the Consecration of the Mass, nothing remains of the bread and wine, but only the appearances, under which Christ, whole and entire, in His "physical reality" is bodily present.

We believe that the Eucharistic Sacrifice or Mass is a permanent institution of the New Testament by the mandate of Christ on that Holy Thursday night, "Do this in remembrance of me" (Lk. 22:19; 1 Cor. 11:24).

Pledge of Christ's Immense Love

Your divine Son, O God, instituted the sacrifice of the Mass at the Last Supper, when, with the words of institution, He showed the sacrificial character of the Eucharist. He said: "This is my body which *is given* for you," (Lk. 22:19), thus designating His body a sacrificial body; and, "This is my blood of the covenant, which *is poured out* for many..." (Mk. 14:24), thus designating His blood as sacrificial blood.

The double Consecration in the Mass is a true representation of the historical, real separation consummated on the cross. To this external act of oblation corresponds an inner act of oblation, in which Christ offers Himself to You,

O Father, as He did on the cross, with those same sacrificial dispositions, in obedience and love, for the forgiveness of our sins.

Your Catholic Church, O God, has always devoutly guarded as a most precious treasure the ineffable gift of the Eucharist as sacrament and as sacrifice, as a pledge of Christ's immense love. During the Second Vatican Council, the Church in a new language spoke again about the institution of the sacrifice of the Mass:

"At the Last Supper, on the night He was handed over, our Lord instituted the Eucharistic Sacrifice of His body and blood, to perpetuate the Sacrifice of the cross throughout the ages until He should come, and thus entrust to the Church, His beloved spouse, the memorial of His death and resurrection..." *(Sacrosanctum concilium, no. 47).*

The Apostles carried on the mandate of Christ. In the apostolic document, the *Didache*, we read the dispositions that one should bring to this sacrifice, which is compared to the sacrifice prophesied by Malachi:

"The sacrifice is that of which the Lord said,
'Everywhere they bring sacrifice to my name....
For great is my name among the nations.
For a great King am I, says the Lord of hosts,
   and my name will be feared among the nations' (Mal. 1:11, 14)."

Yes, O God, You spoke through the prophet Malachi to the Jewish priests about the abolition of their sacrifices and You foretold a new, clean sacrifice.

"I have no pleasure in you, says the Lord of hosts, and I will not accept an offering from your hand. For from the rising of the sun to its setting my name is great among the nations, and in every place incense is offered to my name, and a pure offering; for my name is great among the nations, says the Lord of hosts" (Mal. 1:10-11).

This prophecy was fulfilled in the holy sacrifice of the Mass, which is offered to You, O God, in all parts of the world, and which also, in view of the Victim, Christ Himself, and of the primary sacrificing Priest, Christ Himself, is a clean oblation.

Belief of First Christians

In the Acts of the Apostles we read that those who received the Good News of salvation, preached by the Apostles, were baptized and "devoted themselves to the apostles' teaching and fellowship, to the breaking of bread and the prayers..., praising God and having favor with all the people" (Acts 2:42, 47). From that time on, Your Church has always celebrated the Paschal Mystery by following the same method in the celebration of the sacrifice of the Mass.

St. Irenaeus writes: "The flesh and blood of Christ are the new sacrifices of the new covenant, which have been handed down to the Church by the Apostles, and which she, throughout the whole world, offers to God."

St. Cyprian writes: "The priest who does that which Christ did, truly takes the place of

Christ, and offers in the Church a true and perfect sacrifice to God the Father."

St. Augustine calls the mysterious replica of the sacrifice of the cross, "the daily sacrifice of the Church." The words of the liturgy themselves after the Consecration refer to the nature of the Mass as sacrifice:

"Father, calling to mind the death your Son endured for our salvation,
his glorious resurrection and ascension into heaven,
and ready to greet him when he comes again,
we offer you in thanksgiving this holy and living sacrifice.

"Look with favor on your Church's offering,
and see the Victim whose death has reconciled us to yourself.

"Grant that we, who are nourished by his body and blood,
may be filled with his Holy Spirit,
and become one body, one spirit in Christ.

"May he make us an everlasting gift to you
and enable us to share in the inheritance of your saints....

"Lord, may this sacrifice,
which has made our peace with you,
advance the peace and salvation of all the world."

Eucharistic Prayer III

In the Person of Christ

Father, You want "true worshipers," and by giving us this sacrifice Your Son made it possible for us to worship You in a most worthy way.

"The celebration of the Eucharist," writes Pope John Paul II in *Dominicae cenae*, "has a long history, a history as long as that of the Church. In the course of this history the secondary elements have undergone certain changes, *but there has been no change in the essence of the 'Mysterium'* instituted by the Redeemer of the world at the Last Supper.... For it is He who, represented by the celebrant, makes His entrance into the sanctuary and proclaims His Gospel. It is He who is 'the offerer and the offered, the consecrator and the consecrated.'

"The priest offers the holy Sacrifice *in persona Christi.... In persona* means in specific sacramental identification with 'the eternal High Priest' who is the author and principal subject of this sacrifice of His, a sacrifice in which, in truth, nobody can take His place. Only He—only Christ—was able and is always able to be the true and effective 'expiation for our sins and...for the sins of the whole world'....

"This sacred rite admits of no 'profane' imitation, an imitation that would very easily (indeed regularly) become a profanation.... Therefore the ministers of the Eucharist must, especially today, be illumined by the fullness of this living faith, and in its light they must understand and perform all that is part, by Christ's will and the will of His Church, of their priestly ministry" (no. 8).

Not a few people today, O Lord, have unfortunately turned against Your Church because of this lack of sacredness, witnessed on some occasions.

Consequently, the Pope, aware of this, continues with practical norms:

"The priest cannot consider himself a 'proprietor' who can make free use of the liturgical text and of the sacred rite as if it were his own property, in such a way as to stamp it with his own arbitrary personal style. At times this latter might seem more effective, and it may better correspond to subjective piety; nevertheless, objectively it is always a betrayal of that union which should find its proper expression in the sacrament of unity.

"Every priest who offers the holy Sacrifice should recall that during this Sacrifice it is not only he with his community that is praying but the whole Church, which is thus expressing in this sacrament her spiritual unity, among other ways by the use of the approved liturgical text. To call this position 'mere insistence on uniformity' would only show ignorance of the objective requirements of authentic unity, and would be a symptom of harmful individualism.

"This subordination of the minister, of the celebrant, to the *Mysterium* which has been entrusted to him by the Church for the good of the whole People of God, should also find expression in the observance of the liturgical requirements concerning the celebration of the holy Sacrifice. These refer, for example, to dress, and in particular to the vestments worn by the celebrant. Circumstances have of course existed and continue to exist in which the prescriptions do not oblige. We have been greatly moved when reading books written by priests who had been prisoners in extermination camps, with descriptions of Eucharistic Celebrations without the above-mentioned rules, that is to say, without an altar and without vestments. But although in those conditions this was a proof of heroism and deserved profound admiration, nevertheless in normal conditions to ignore the liturgical directives can be interpreted as a lack of respect towards the Eucharist, dictated perhaps by individualism or by an absence of a critical sense concerning current opinions, or by a certain lack of spirit of faith....

"It must always be remembered that only the Word of God can be used for Mass readings. The reading of Scripture cannot be replaced by the reading of other texts, however much they may be endowed with undoubted religious and moral values. On the other hand such texts can be used very profitably in the homily" (nos. 12, 10).

Changes of Vatican II

Other people, Lord, have mistakenly abandoned this sacrifice of our salvation, the Mass, because of the changes brought about by Vatican II: for example, the vernacular in place of Latin, the Offertory procession, extraordinary ministers, etc. The words of Pope John Paul II in *Dominicae cenae* are words of understanding:

"We should remember that these changes demand new spiritual awareness and maturity, both on the part of the celebrant—especially now that he celebrates 'facing the people'—and by the faithful.

"We are well aware that from the earliest times the celebration of the Eucharist has been linked not only with prayer but also with the reading of Sacred Scripture and with singing by the whole assembly....

"The insertion of the Psalms with responses into the liturgy makes the participants familiar with the great wealth of Old Testament prayer and poetry. The fact that these texts are read and sung in the vernacular enables everyone to participate with fuller understanding" (nos. 9, 10).

At this point we hear from the heart of the Pope his message in favor of those who have a great love for that splendid language, Latin. He says in the same document:

"There are also those people who, having been educated on the basis of the old liturgy in Latin, experience the lack of this 'one language,' which in all the world was an expression of the unity of the Church and through its dignified character elicited a profound sense of the Eucharistic Mystery. It is therefore necessary to show not only understanding but also full respect towards these sentiments and desires. As far as possible these sentiments and desires are to be accommodated, as is moreover provided for in the new dispositions" (no. 10).

A word of explanation is important here for those who remain attached to the Tridentine Latin Mass and refuse the new Latin Mass as approved by Pope Paul VI.

Logically speaking, O Lord, these objectors should reason that one Pope has the same authority as another. And in matters of rites in the liturgy, not substance, both of them have the same authority, which should be respected by the faithful.

He Died for All

Unfortunately, O God, these are also the same persons who criticize the Mass in the vernacular, especially because of the way the Latin words of the Consecration are translated into English. The Latin *"pro multis"* in English is rendered: "for *all* men," while it is pointed out that literally the word "multis" means "many." But we know that holy Mother Church, through Vatican Council II, felt the need to restore and promote the sacred liturgy for the purpose of making it more understandable to Your People, in order that the Eucharistic Sacrifice would be more profitable, our Faith be better nourished, our minds raised to You, our spiritual homage increased, and our hearts be filled more abundantly with Your grace.

Hence the changing of the translation of *multis* (many) into *all* was done so that its explicit meaning, according to the Bible, would be given. For "many" is a Semitic way of saying "for everybody" or "all."

O God, make these objectors see that this translation is legitimate. In fact, the mission of Your Son is to save *all*, as St. Paul, too, wrote: "He (Christ) died for all..." (2 Cor. 5:15). And to Timothy, he wrote: "Christ Jesus...gave himself as a ransom for all" (1 Tm. 2:5-6). To the Romans he said: "As one man's trespass led to condemnation for all men, so one man's act of righteousness leads to acquittal and life for all men" (Rom. 5:18).

O God, send Your Holy Spirit upon those who take it upon themselves to interpret Your revelation. You entrusted this interpretation to the Church founded by Your Son, commanding that she teach us only and everything which Your Son, our Lord Jesus Christ taught, without omission or error.

When we speak about the sacrifice of the Mass, O Lord, we have no words to thank Your divine Son for this greatest of gifts. In fact, so many are the advantages of the sacrifice of the Mass that if we knew them all, the churches would be full to overflowing—and not only on Sundays and holydays of obligation, but every day.

The Saving Power of the Mass

One last thing to be treated concerning the sacrifice of the Mass is its saving power applied to our souls. In it the fruits of the sacrifice of the cross are applied to us.

In no way does the Mass detract from the sacrifice of the cross. Rather it draws its whole power from that very sacrifice of the cross, and applies its fruits to individual persons. As the purpose of the sacrifice of Jesus on the cross was primarily the adoration or glorification of You, Father, and secondarily our thanksgiving, expiation, and petition, so it is in the Mass. In fact, in every Mass Your Son Jesus Christ uses the human priest only as His representative. But it is He who performs the actual, immediate sacrificial action.

Often even today some churches, whether in the city or country, have early Masses attended by many devout persons. They are working people, business men and women, housewives as well as young people. Fervently they receive daily Holy Communion. They know that by going to Holy Communion they participate more fully in the sacrifice, since they receive sacramentally the Victim of the sacrifice, Jesus. In doing so, they share in Your life and realize a union with all Your people, so that their Christian life becomes more and more evident.

It was, in fact, for this purpose that Your Son entrusted His sacrifice to the Church so that the participants might share in it spiritually by faith and love, and sacramentally through Holy Communion. Here we all feel united with our brethren both in the local and universal Church, and not only with them, but with all humanity, because in the sacrifice of the Mass, Christ offers Himself for the salvation of the entire world. As a consequence, people who are faithful to participation at Mass grow in Christian perfection, since they are cleansed from sin and strengthened to live for You, O God, and their neighbor, through works of charity, of mutual help, and various forms of activity as Christian witnesses.

A tragic fact is still happening today, O Lord: people who abandon the Mass because they claim that their priest is an unworthy minister. So they deprive themselves and their dear ones, living and deceased, of this sacrifice of expiation which effects the remission of sins, and the punishment due for sin, and confers supernatural and natural gifts. St. Paul says: "Every high priest chosen from among men is appointed to act on behalf of men in relation to God, to offer gifts and sacrifices for sins" (Heb. 5:1).

For the consolation of these people, the truth is that the sacrifice of the Mass works independently of the moral worthiness of the celebrating priest, because it is the self-sacrifice of Christ, who is the principal Priest, and it is the sacrifice of the Church to which it was transmitted by Christ.

The human priest is only the servant and the representative of Christ, as St. Paul says:

"This is how one should regard us, as servants of Christ and stewards of the mysteries of God" (1 Cor. 4:1).

"We are ambassadors for Christ, God making his appeal through us" (2 Cor. 5:20).

What definitely is to be considered is the truth that the measure of the punishment of sins remitted is, in the case of the living, proportional to the degree of perfection of their dispositions. When the Mass is offered for the souls in purgatory, as they are in the state of grace and thus have no obstacle, it is believed that at least part of their punishment is infallibly remitted. Beautiful, therefore, and to be retained is the custom of offering Masses in memory of dear ones and friends departed from this life.

Yes, the value of the sacrifice of the Mass in itself is infinite because of the infinite dignity of the Victim, Your Son Jesus Christ, and because of the principal sacrificial Priest, again Your Son Jesus Christ. And it is worthy of You, O infinite God, because it is an infinite sacrifice.

For us, finite human beings, the sacrifice has finite effects only, and this is the reason the Church offers the holy sacrifice of the Mass frequently even for the same intention.

The best way to receive the maximum fruits of the Mass is to live a holy life. Then we can unite ourselves with the priest in all his prayers, recited with humility and faith.

O Lord, help us to appreciate ever more fully the tremendous treasure we possess in Your gift to us of the Eucharistic Sacrifice.

Your love makes You dwell in the holy Tabernacle, renew Your passion in the Mass and give Yourself to us as food for our souls in holy Communion. May we know You, O hidden God! May we draw saving waters from the font of Your Heart. Grant us the grace to visit You often, even every day in this Sacrament, to understand and actively participate in holy Mass, to receive holy Communion frequently and with the right dispositions.

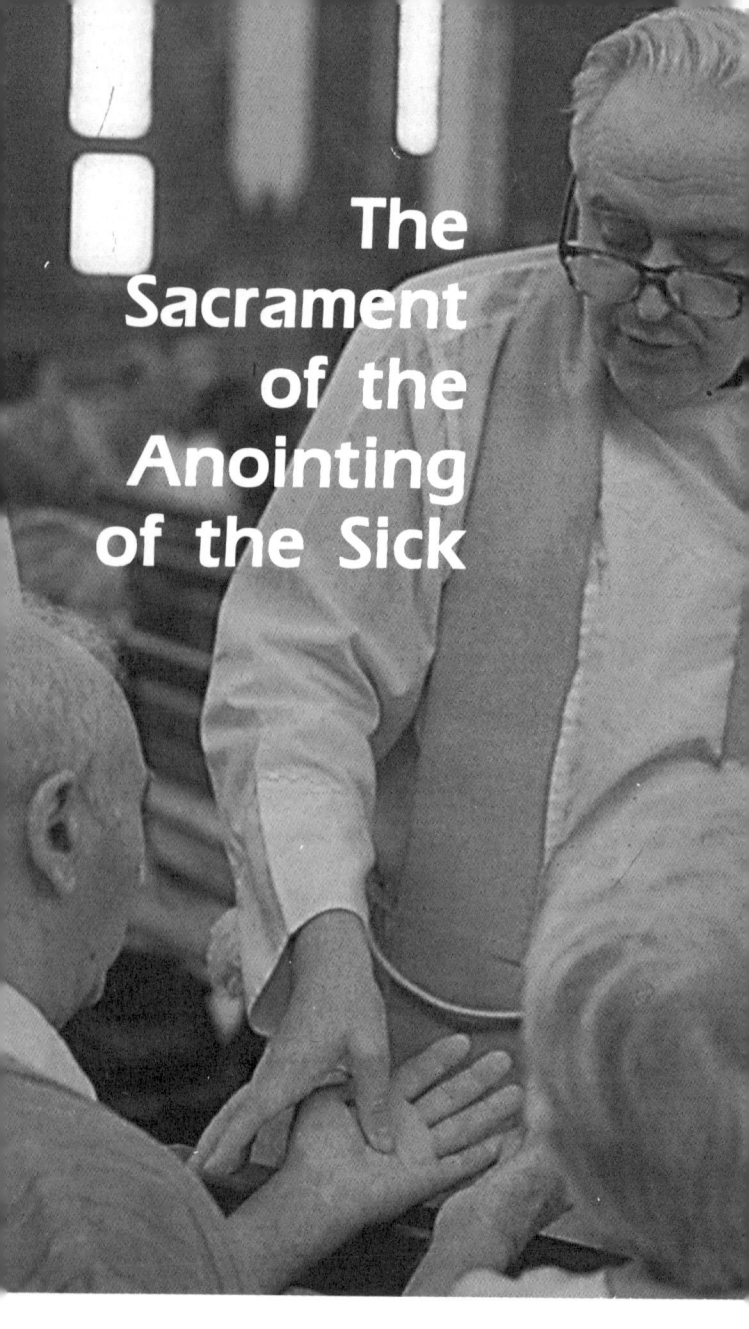

The Sacrament of the Anointing of the Sick

A great change has taken place in our day, O Lord. Groups of old people come to our churches with devout dispositions to receive the sacrament of the Anointing of the Sick.

Your Church obeys the command of Your Son to cure the sick: "And these signs will accompany those who believe: ...they will lay their hands on the sick, and they will recover" (Mk. 16:17, 18). Your Church follows the example of our Lord Jesus, who "went about doing good and healing..." (Acts 10:38).

The Anointing of the Sick is one of the seven sacraments instituted by Your Son to show His love for the sick—He who so often during His life looked upon them and healed them. The Gospel alludes to this sacrament when it says: "And they (the Twelve) cast out many demons, and anointed with oil many that were sick and healed them" (Mk. 6:13).

Your apostle St. James described it and promulgated it to the faithful:

"Is any among you sick? Let him call for the elders of the church, and let them pray over him, anointing him with oil in the name of the Lord; and the prayer of faith will save the sick man, and the Lord will raise him up; and if he has committed sins, he will be forgiven" (Jas. 5:14-15).

In the ancient Church, of both East and West, we find the use of this sacrament. The effects of this sacrament are: forgiveness of venial sins, and also mortal sins (even forgotten ones) if the recipient is sorry for them, but unable to confess them; it also remits at least some of the temporal punishment still due for sin; it communicates grace, relieves and strengthens the soul of the sick person by arousing in him or her a great confidence in Your divine mercy; it helps to bear more easily the trials and hardships of sickness; it gives strength for resisting the temptations of the devil; and sometimes it even helps one to regain health if this is expedient for the good of the soul.

What care You have for Your children, O God. You have provided for them Baptism to begin life; You accompany them through the journey of life with the sacraments of Confirmation, Penance and Holy Eucharist; You gave to them the sacraments of Matrimony and Holy Orders for the good of society; and, finally, You provided a sacrament to close one's life holily.

But this sacrament of the Anointing of the Sick is not only for those who are at the point of death. It can be received as soon as any one of the faithful begins to be in danger of death from sickness or old age.

The priest administers this sacrament by anointing the person on the forehead and hands with blessed oil, while saying this prayer:

"Through this holy anointing
may the Lord in his love and mercy help you
with the grace of the Holy Spirit.   R. Amen.
May the Lord who frees you from sin
save you and raise you up.   R. Amen."

Rite of Anointing

Another grace is to be able to receive this sacrament more than once in the course of the same illness if the danger becomes more serious, or if the sick person recovers and then falls ill again. How much easier it is, then, to offer one's sufferings to You, in union with Christ's sufferings. St. Paul says:

"This slight momentary affliction is preparing for us an eternal weight of glory beyond all comparison..." (2 Cor. 4:17).

We want to thank You, O Father, for having provided us and our dear ones with the strongest means of support at the time when our soul needs to be saved from eternal damnation and to be raised up from discouragement or even despair.

May relatives and friends consider their duty to do whatever they can to help the sick not only physically but also, and especially, spiritually. As soon as they see the need, may they provide for them the physical relief necessary, and above all the spiritual comfort.

The Sacrament of Holy Orders

For the spiritual benefit of Your People, O God, Your Son Jesus Christ, Our Lord and Savior, instituted also another sacrament—the sacrament of Holy Orders.

With this sacrament is given to one of Your faithful, by the imposition of the bishop's hands and the prayer, a special seal of the Holy Spirit to attend to Your ministry, O God, for the benefit of Your Church.

By this sacrament, priests are appointed to take an active part in Christ's priesthood, by sharing in that ministry of salvation that our Savior accomplished in the world. In fact, after ordination, priests become obliged to dispense the saving treasures of Christ and to lead a morally pure life. They are called to live closer to Christ and to be His witnesses in the world. They are to share the burden of their brothers and sisters, and strengthen their faith by word and example. They are to teach the Gospel and gather the faithful together to share in the Eucharistic Sacrifice.

Lord, fill Your priests with the spirit of Your love, so that they may always be the salt that purifies, the light of the world, the city placed on the mountaintop.

To them Your Son entrusted the treasure of His doctrine, of His law, of His grace, and souls themselves. May we all love them, listen to them, and let ourselves be guided on the paths leading to heaven.

According to Your Holy Bible, the Apostles or their disciples who had been consecrated bishops were the only ministers for the ordination of deacons, priests and bishops. The Acts of the Apostles recounts the ordination of seven deacons:

"These they set before the apostles, and they prayed and laid their hands upon them" (Acts 6:6).

And in the Acts we also read that Paul and Barnabas "appointed elders (priests) for them in every church, with prayer and fasting, they committed them to the Lord in whom they believed" (Acts 14:23).

St. Paul, in writing to Timothy, says:

"I remind you to rekindle the gift of God that is within you through the laying on of my hands" (2 Tm. 1:6).

And again to Timothy he exhorts:

"Do not be hasty in the laying on of hands..." (1 Tm. 5:22).

To Titus the Apostle says:

"This is why I left you in Crete, that you might amend what was defective, and appoint elders in every town as I directed you" (Ti. 1:5).

Ordination of Women?

One thing that today especially should be recalled, O Lord, is the fact that only men have been ordained priests from the time of the earliest Christian Church. Christ Himself called only men to the apostolate, and throughout the history of the Church the sacrament of Holy Orders has been handed on to men only.

Bear with us, Lord, if we spend a little time in giving a convincing answer to those who object.

The mandate of Your Son, Jesus Christ, on Holy Thursday, when He instituted the sacrament of Holy Orders at the Last Supper, was addressed exclusively to the Apostles and to their successors. He said: "Do this in remembrance of me" (Lk. 22:19; 1 Cor. 11:24).

The official document of the Sacred Congregation for the Doctrine of the Faith, *Declaration on the Question of the Admission of Women to the Ministerial Priesthood*, says:

"The Attitude of Christ: Jesus Christ did not call any woman to become part of the Twelve. If He acted in this way, it was not in order to conform to the customs of His time, for His attitude towards women was quite different from that of His milieu, and He deliberately and courageously broke with it....

"Even His Mother, who was so closely associated with the mystery of her Son, and whose incomparable role is emphasized by the Gospels of Luke and John, was not invested with the apostolic ministry. This fact was to lead the Fathers to present her as the example of Christ's will in this domain....

"The Practice of the Apostles: The apostolic community remained faithful to the attitude of Jesus towards women. Although Mary occupied a privileged place in the little circle of those gathered in the Upper Room after the Lord's Ascension (cf. Acts 1:14), it was not she who was called to enter the College of the Twelve at the time of the election that resulted in the choice of Matthias: those who were put forward were two disciples whom the Gospels do not even mention.

"On the day of Pentecost, the Holy Spirit filled them all, men and women (cf. Acts 2:1; 1:14), yet the proclamation of the fulfillment of the prophecies in Jesus was made only by 'Peter and the Eleven' (Acts 2:14).

"When they (the Apostles) and Paul went beyond the confines of the Jewish world, the preaching of the Gospel and the Christian life in the Greco-Roman civilization impelled them to break with Mosaic practices, sometimes regretfully. They could therefore have envisaged conferring ordination on women, if they had not been convinced of their duty of fidelity to the Lord on this point. In the Hellenistic world, the cult of a number of pagan divinities was entrusted to priestesses. In fact, the Greeks did not share the ideas of the Jews: although their philosophers taught the inferiority of women, historians nevertheless emphasize the existence of a certain movement for the advancement of women during the Imperial period. In fact, we know from the book of the Acts and from the Letters of St. Paul that certain women worked with the Apostle for the Gospel (cf. Rom. 16:3-12; Phil. 4:3). St. Paul lists their names with gratitude in the final salutations of the Letters. Some of them often exercised an important influence on conversions: Priscilla, Lydia and others; especially Priscilla, who took it on herself to complete the instruction of Apollos (cf. Acts 18:26); Phoebe, in the service of the Church of Cenchreae (cf. Rom. 16:1). All these facts manifest within the Apostolic Church a considerable evolution vis-à-vis the customs of

Judaism. Nevertheless at no time was there a question of conferring ordination on these women....

"Could the Church today depart from this attitude of Jesus and the Apostles, which has been considered as normative by the whole of tradition up to our own day?"

St. Paul and Women

O God, in regard to St. Paul, objections are raised about some of his prescriptions concerning women. But these prescriptions are nothing else but disciplinary norms about practices of minor importance, such as the obligation imposed on women to wear veils, a convention probably inspired by the custom of that period (1 Cor. 11:2-16).

What St. Paul forbids to women is of an altogether different nature, that is, the official function of teaching in the Christian assembly (cf. 1 Cor. 14:34-35; 1 Tm. 2:12), while instead he in no way opposes women's right to prophesy in the assembly (cf. 1 Cor. 11:5).

The above-cited document concludes this matter thus:

"Nor should it be forgotten that we owe to St. Paul one of the most vigorous texts in the New Testament on the fundamental equality of men and women, as children of God in Christ (cf. Gal. 3:28). Therefore there is no reason for accusing him of prejudices against women, when we note the trust that he shows towards them and the collaboration that he asks of them in his apostolate."

Yes, there were deaconesses in the early Christian Church. They were consecrated with a special rite including imposition of hands and prayer, and they formed a definite rank, but they never were allowed to exercise priestly functions. Their principal duties were to assist at the Baptism of women and to care for the poor and the sick.

A Life for Others

O God, may each woman recognize herself as a true follower of Christ when she works not for herself alone, but for others as well. Let her fulfill herself by following in the footsteps of the great women of history.

It has been said that "whoever has charge of the formation of young girls can truly say that he or she controls the future destiny of the world." This is so because there is much good that women can do to transform society. They can oppose whatever tends to disrupt the family, which is the nucleus of society. They can contribute much toward the condemnation of divorce, "free love," and all forms of immorality. With their love, they can take an effective, active part in moral and religious matters, such as sustaining their husbands and children with a spirit of loving solicitude; giving religious instruction; promoting the Catholic press and wholesome media programs; organizing conferences; and, if financially able, by sustaining worthwhile projects.

One of the many examples in our time is the following. Two girls, in their early twenties, wanted to do something about the evil of abortion. But what could they do—two young girls—on their own? They thought about it, then talked it over. They had little money to finance any special undertaking, but their good will was strong. Soon enough they began. Began what? A small pro-life office to help women contemplating abortion. Yes, "where there is the will, there is the way." Every good work, no matter how small, contributes to building up a better world.

Our world needs greatly these dedicated women, O Lord. Therefore, it is a pity when one sees too many talents used for purposes which are useless—for time and for eternity.

May the names of Judith, Ruth, Bridget, Monica, Elizabeth of Hungary, Anne Marie Taigi, Catherine of Siena, Teresa of Avila, Theresa of Lisieux, Pauline Jaricot, Mary Mazzarello, Mother Seton, Mother Thecla Merlo and millions of others—girls, mothers, widows, contemplative and active religious—and especially Mary, Your holy Mother and handmaid, O God—be of constant inspiration to the woman of today, in the world of today, which is so much in need of a woman's intuition, sensitivity and faith!

The Sacrament of Holy Matrimony

The Lord God...brought [the woman] to [Adam]. Then the man said,
"This at last is bone of my bones
and flesh of my flesh;
she shall be called Woman,
because she was taken out of Man."
Therefore a man leaves his father and his mother and cleaves to his wife, and they become one flesh.

God blessed them, and God said to them, "Be fruitful and multiply" (Gn. 2:22-24; 1:28).

Marriage was not instituted by man, but by You, O God. You created mankind as men and women (Gn. 1:27), blessed the first human pair and revealed to them Your mandate of reproduction (Gn. 1:28).

"Man," comments Pope John Paul II, "in the first beautifying meeting, finds the woman and she finds him. In this way man accepts her interiorly; he accepts her as she is willed 'for her own sake' by the Creator as she is constituted in the mystery of the image of God through her femininity; and, reciprocally, she accepts man in the same way, as he is willed 'for his own sake' by the Creator, and constituted by Him by means of his masculinity. The revelation and the discovery of the *mystery* meaning of the body consists in this."

Your eternal love, O Lord, created man and woman to love each other. The first idyllic love which blossomed in the earthly paradise under Your gaze has been followed by millions and millions of others in the world. And each time Your gaze has rested on men and women to bless their love, which is a participation in divine love itself.

Married love is a blessed exchange, a source of living water in which a couple can satisfy their thirst for joy and happiness and realize the miracle of life in giving each other children. In Matrimony, they promise each other this love, solemnly exchanging rights to their hearts and bodies. They oblige themselves to reserve for each other all their affection and to love each other only, more than their very parents, each considering the other as another self.

A great mystery, indeed, is human love.

Your Son, Jesus Christ brought marriage back again to the way You had ordained it—that is, to that original indissoluble monogamy—and elevated it to the dignity of a sacrament:

"'And Pharisees came up to him and tested him by asking, 'Is it lawful to divorce one's wife for any cause?' He answered, 'Have you not read that he who made them from the beginning made them male and female, and said, "For this reason a man shall leave his father and mother and be joined to his wife, and the two shall become one"? So they are no longer two but one. What therefore God has joined together, let no man put asunder.' They said to him, 'Why then did Moses command one to give a certificate of divorce, and to put her away?' He said to them, 'For your hardness of heart Moses allowed you to divorce your wives, but from the beginning it was not so' " (Mt. 19:3-8).

"Hence," comments Vatican II, "by that human act, whereby spouses mutually bestow and accept each other, a relationship arises which by divine will and in the eyes of society too is a lasting one. For the good of the spouses and their offspring as well as of society, the existence of the sacred bond no longer depends on human decisions alone. For God Himself is the Author of Matrimony, endowed as it is with various benefits and purposes. All of these have a very decisive bearing on the continuation of the human race, on the personal development and eternal destiny of the individual members of a family, and on the dignity, stability, peace and prosperity of the family itself and of human society as a whole" *(Gaudium et spes*, no. 48).

Lasting Love

After the funeral of his eighty-year-old wife, a widower, 87, did not lose his faith in life. Speaking to a friend of his, he said honestly, "I'm determined to keep up my courage. There is one thing that helps me do this and is of great comfort to me: I remained faithful to my wife for sixty years."

True love never grows old. The love of a couple who were joined in Your presence, O Lord, becomes a walk toward perfection, over a road not yet paved but smoothed by sanctifying and sacramental grace, which daily makes husband and wife capable of a greater love, unifying and fruitful.

Your apostle Paul points out the religious character of marriage among Christians and proclaims its indissolubility, as commanded by the Lord: "A wife is bound to her husband as long as he lives. If the husband dies, she is free to be married to whom she wishes, only in the Lord" (1 Cor. 7:39).

He also adds: "To the married I give charge, not I but the Lord, that the wife should not separate from her husband (but if she does, let her remain single or else be reconciled to her husband)—and that the husband should not divorce his wife" (1 Cor. 7:10-11).

He compares the dignity and sanctity of Christian marriage to Christ's love for His Church. As the unity of Christ with His Church is a great source of grace for the members of the Church, so Matrimony communicates much grace because it is a sacrament: " 'For this reason a man shall leave his father and mother and be joined to his wife, and the two shall become one.' This is a great mystery, and I mean in reference to Christ and the church; however, let each one of you love his wife as himself, and let the wife see that she respects her husband" (Eph. 5:31-33).

How important, O Lord, is this mutual respect between husband and wife. I recall the story of a young bride who, two weeks after the wedding, found herself confronted with a shocking episode. A very good young woman, she was busily preparing supper when her husband came home. He entered the kitchen, greeted her, then showed her a very immoral magazine.

"My reaction was immediate," she said. "I took the magazine from the table on which he had tossed it, put it back in his hands and told him, 'If this is the kind of thing you read, both you and that trash can leave this house.' My heart was pounding as he headed toward the door. But it eased as I saw him go straight to the garbage can outside and throw the magazine in. Never again has a piece of pornographic literature entered our home. And since then we have not only grown in respect for one another, but also in a more intimate love."

This great sacrament of Matrimony communicates that grace which is necessary to carry on a basic purpose—generation and upbringing of children: "And God said to them, 'Be fruitful and multiply...'" (Gn. 1:28); and it also gives the grace to fulfill another purpose—mutual help: "I will make him (man) a helper fit for him" (Gn. 2:18), and the morally regulated satisfaction of the sexual urge: "Because of the temptation to immorality, each man should have his own wife and each woman her own husband. The husband should give to his wife her conjugal rights, and likewise the wife to her husband" (1 Cor. 7:2-3).

Yes, O God, You gave Christian spouses a special sacrament by which they are fortified and can fulfill their conjugal and family obligations with faith, hope and charity. Thus they increasingly advance toward perfection of their own personalities, as well as toward salvation and holiness.

"Sealed by mutual faithfulness," says Vatican II, "and hallowed above all by Christ's sacrament, conjugal love remains steadfastly true in body and in mind, in bright days or dark. It will never be profaned by adultery or divorce. Firmly established by the Lord, the unity of marriage will radiate from the equal personal dignity of wife and husband, a dignity acknowledged by mutual and total love. Graced with the dignity and office of fatherhood and motherhood, parents will energetically acquit themselves of a duty which devolves primarily on them, namely education and especially religious education. The constant fulfillment of the duties of this Christian vocation demands notable virtue. For this reason, strengthened by grace for holiness of life, the couple will painstakingly cultivate and pray for steadiness of love, largeheartedness and the spirit of sacrifice" *(Gaudium et spes,* no. 49).

I recently spent an evening with a couple nearing their eighties. The husband is very sociable and, in fact, quite talkative. The wife is pleasant, composed and a very good listener.

"In six months we'll be celebrating our sixtieth wedding anniversary," the husband said, and then he began recounting some memories of their long life together. They were beautiful memories, often humorous, and at times painful, as for instance during the Depression.

"Yes, we have had our share of fights. I have to admit I've raised my voice during them, too. But soon enough, one or the other of us apologizes and the disagreement ends with a kiss."

Statistics affirm that in the United States, one out of every two marriages ends in divorce. What are the causes? Many. However, there are still many couples who faithfully live their vocation. One such couple, already in their sixties, are very happy in their married life. They are persons with their own viewpoint, but both communicate and dialogue about their opinions. When asked by a visiting friend if they ever argue, the husband replied, "Yes, we do occasionally. And generally I have the last word." His strong character was obvious, even in his tone of voice. "But," he added immediately, as his wife sat by smiling, "the arguments last no more than five minutes because," he said with a broad smile, pointing to his wife, "she tells me pleasantly, 'By the way, you didn't say you're sorry yet....' " Then he added with a chuckle, "I can't resist her smile or her manner, so I only answer, 'But I didn't start it—you did.' And the whole thing ends that way."

Every marriage is meant to be the realization of a deep friendship between a man and a woman, an exchange of interests, of ideals, of aspirations, of intellectual, spiritual and social plans. Among the sincere friendships he cultivates, a man must make his wife his best friend, and her husband should be a woman's closest friend. This genuine friendship will save the matrimonial partnership from the hard knocks dealt it by its surroundings and the passing of time.

Union of spirit is the secret of enduring friendship in marriage, which the gift of the physical self seals. "They were one not only in flesh but above all in spirit," reads the epitaph of one good couple. "You and Mom," wrote a man to his father, "are two people who form one person for me. Whenever you told me something, Dad, I knew beforehand that it would be something Mom had told me also. Honestly, Dad, I think the Lord formed a union of soul, spirit and heart between you and Mom."

Once the proverbial "I do" has been uttered, the partners get ready to shoulder their yoke, with divine grace. But You, O Lord, have promised that Your yoke is sweet and Your burden light.

"I love you," the groom declares as he slips the blessed ring onto the finger of the woman of his choice. That ring is symbolic of the knot which has irrevocably joined their lives.

I love and want you forever. This is no mere secret promise. It is public, taken before You, O Lord, and before Your people.

A woman already advanced in years wrote to her husband: "Peter, I was so happy to hear you tell me again that I shall be your love for all eternity. My heart is young and full of life, but my strength is slowly leaving me. Still, I'm full of courage."

This is fidelity. And fidelity means love.

True love demands loving until the end. It cannot bear the thought of separation from the loved one.

Why, then, is the divorce rate and dissension so high?

"For your hardness of heart," said Christ, "Moses allowed you to divorce your wives" (Mt. 19:8). We're not living in Moses' day, and Christ does not permit divorce.

The only solution to certain impossible family situations is *separation*, temporary or even permanent, but without the possibility of remarriage, for the marriage bond is broken only by death: "What God has joined together, let no man put asunder" (Mt. 19:6).

Fidelity requires self-control and a spirit of sacrifice. This self-control, in turn, means constant effort and, above all, love and faithfulness to You, my God. No longer should the "I" predominate; rather, it should be replaced by the "we." Jesus said clearly:

"For this reason a man shall leave his father and mother and be joined to his wife, and the two shall become one. So they are no longer two but one" (Mt. 19:5-6).

A good book for husbands and wives to read is the magnificent book on Matrimony in the

Bible—*Tobit*. They can make their own the prayer and noble sentiments of Sarah and Tobias before they came together as man and wife.

Tobias exhorted the virgin, and said to her, "Sister, get up, and let us pray that the Lord may have mercy upon us." And Tobias began to pray,

"Blessed are you, O God of our fathers,
    and blessed be your holy and glorious name for ever.
    Let the heavens and all your creatures bless you.
You made Adam and gave him Eve his wife as a helper and support....
"And now, O Lord, I am not taking this sister of mine because of lust, but with sincerity. Grant that I may find mercy and may grow old together with her" (Tob. 8:4-7).

Parenthood

With such sentiments, husband and wife will have the grace to give themselves to each other without frustrating the sacred acts of love, without disturbing by selfishness the joy of their union.

Give, O Lord, to husband and wife the courage and strength needed to avoid selfishness. May they commit themselves permanently to respecting the purpose You gave both of them at the dawn of creation: "Be fruitful and multiply" (Gn. 1:28).

A child is the wonderful fruit of the intimate cooperation of parental love with Your love, O Lord. In the psalms, You tell us that children are Your gift, the reward and the fruit of love.

May the first child come soon, then—this little creature who will seal wedded love and bring it to its full realization! Love, however, wills to keep expressing itself. The home that always welcomes children is a home where You, O Lord, carry out Your promise of happiness.

Just last week, Susan, nearly four, was in bed, when she heard her father and mother having a small quarrel in the next room. When their raised voices quieted down, and they were also in bed, Susan's little voice broke the deep silence. "Mommy, Daddy, is everything okay now?" The answer came, "Yes, Honey, everything's all right." In a flash the youngster jumped out of bed and ran into her parents' room. She gave each a big hug and kiss, then went back to bed.

Founded on love, the family must be ruled by love. Parental authority must be like Yours, Lord—a loving service to the children.

The Second Vatican Council spoke of the important role of parents: "The family is a kind of school of deeper humanity. But if it is to achieve the full flowering of its life and mission, it needs the kindly communion of minds and the joint deliberation of spouses, as well as the painstaking cooperation of parents in the education of their children. The active presence of the father is highly beneficial to their formation. The children, especially the younger among them, need the care of their mother at home. This domestic role of hers must be safely preserved, though the legitimate social progress of women should not be underrated on that account" *(Gaudium et spes*, no. 52).

There are couples even in our own day who, while serving society, still take direct care of their own children, without entrusting them to babysitters or institutions.

One such couple I know both practice their teaching profession in a large university. Who cares for their four young children, aged eight, six, four and seven months? "We ourselves do, taking turns, teaching classes on alternating days. We are determined to raise our own children and not leave them in the hands of others. Through this togetherness we have grown closer in many ways and our happiness daily increases."

Children need to be made to feel that they are the fruit of a love freely, joyously given and accepted. They must be able to breathe in an atmosphere of warmth and serenity in their own home, so that they grow up with confidence in themselves and in others. Discipline, too, is needed, however, as You have said:

"Do not withhold discipline from a child....
Train up a child in the way he should go,
  and when he is old he will not depart from it.
The father of the righteous will greatly rejoice;
  he who begets a wise son will be glad in him"
    (Prv. 23:13, 22:6, 23:24).

May the child see in his father a model and guide to follow! May he see in his mother treasures of goodness and love. What a marvelous mission fatherhood and motherhood constitute! And when the children leave home, the love of husband and wife, ever increased by faith, will make each dearer than ever to the other. This love of theirs, now stronger and surer, deeper and firmer, will be with them until they reach the eternal Home where human love made sublime is joined to Your own love, my God, forever and ever.

"Let the Children Come to Me"

Now Adam knew Eve his wife, and she conceived and bore Cain, saying, "I have gotten a man with the help of the Lord." And again, she bore his brother Abel (Gn. 4:1-2).

To appreciate the greatness of the divine gift of procreation, the blessing of marriage, it is enough to contemplate the dignity of the human person and his sublime destiny. His rational nature sets man above all other visible creatures.

Your purpose, Lord, in willing human beings to be born is not merely that they may exist and occupy the earth, but far more, that they may worship You, and that they may know and love You and finally enjoy You forever in heaven.

This destiny, by reason of man's wondrous elevation to the supernatural order, surpasses everything that eye has seen or ear heard, or the heart of man has been able to conceive. Clearly, therefore, the offspring begotten by Your almighty power with the cooperation of husband and wife is a very noble gift of Your goodness and a most excellent fruit of marriage.

In the family, we see the marvelous, close cooperation of two human persons, created to the divine image and likeness, called to the great mission of continuing and prolonging the creative work, in giving physical life to new beings in whom the life-giving Spirit infuses the powerful principle of immortal life.

"I have gotten a man with the help of the Lord," said Eve. And the heroic mother of the Maccabees said to her sons: "I do not know how you came into being in my womb. It was not I who gave you life and breath, nor I who set in order the elements within each of you. The Creator of the world...shaped the beginning of man..." (2 Mac. 7:22-23).

The child, formed in the womb of his mother, is a gift from You, O God. You confide his care to the parents, to educate and bring up in the fear of You, O God, and in the faith.

May spouses value and appreciate the honor of producing a new life, and await its coming with a holy impatience! Unfortunately, however, this is not always the case; the child is often not wanted; worse still, its coming is often dreaded. Most tragically of all, in millions of cases, the innocent life is snuffed out by abortion.

The Gift of Life

I recall here, Lord, an episode from Your Bible:

"Then the king of Egypt said to the Hebrew midwives, one of whom was named Shiphrah and the other Puah, 'When you serve as midwife to the Hebrew women, and see them upon the birthstool, if it is a son, you shall kill him; but if it is a daughter, she shall live.' But the midwives feared God, and did not do as the king of Egypt commanded them, but let the male children live. So the king of Egypt called the midwives, and said to them, 'Why have you done this, and let the male children live?' The midwives said to Pharaoh, 'Because the Hebrew women are not like the Egyptian women; for they are vigorous and are delivered before the midwife comes to them.' So God dealt well with the midwives; and the people multiplied and grew very strong. And because the midwives feared God he gave them families" (Ex. 1:15-21).

Yes, Lord, life is a great gift. What respect it commands on our part! Your bountiful blessings rained down on the Hebrew midwives because they recognized You alone as the Lord and Master of life. Indeed, the wonderful mystery surrounding the beginning of new human life must lead every thoughtful person to reverence You, O Lord, our Creator, and the laws You have laid down protecting the right to life.

In Your Sacred Book, You teach us respect for human life at every stage of its existence, since every human being comes from You, goes back to You, belongs to You:

"Know that the Lord is God!
  It is he that made us, and we are his"
    (Ps. 100:3).

"For you did form my inward parts,
  you did knit me together in my mother's womb.

I praise you, for you are fearful and wonderful. Wonderful are your works!" (Ps. 139:13-14)

Vatican II spoke strongly and clearly: "For God, the Lord of life, has conferred on men the surpassing ministry of safeguarding life—a ministry which must be fulfilled in a manner which is worthy of man. Therefore, from the moment of its conception, life must be guarded with the greatest care, while abortion and infanticide are unspeakable crimes" *(Gaudium et spes,* no. 51). Even the unborn child is "man" to the same degree and by the same title as the parents.

Furthermore, every human being, even a child in the mother's womb, has a right to life directly from You, O God, and not from the parents or from any human society or authority. Hence there is no man, no human authority, no science, no medical, eugenic, social, economic or moral "indication" that can offer or produce a valid juridical title to a direct deliberate disposal of an innocent human life. That is to say, a disposal that aims at its destruction, whether as an end or as a means to an end, which is, perhaps, in no way unlawful in itself. Thus, for example, to save the life of the mother is a very noble end; but the direct killing of the child as a means to that end is not lawful.

Prayer Insures Fidelity

The violence of rebellious passions is certainly the principal source of sins against the laws of Matrimony. Thus, it follows that the first necessity in those who unite themselves in the sacred bonds of Matrimony is an inner, genuine prayer life, one which will pervade their whole lives and fill mind and will with the deepest reverence for Your divine law, O Lord.

Guard us from the propaganda of what is called "rational birth control" *(planned parenthood)*, supported by individuals and associations, sometimes distinguished for other undertakings, but in this one, unfortunately, they have made a serious mistake.

Let governments and legislatures, O Lord, remember that it is the duty of public authority to protect the lives of the innocent by appropriate laws and penalties, especially when those whose lives are attacked and endangered are unable to protect themselves, as is particularly the case with infants in their mother's womb.

May we never forget that there rises, above every man-made law, Your law, O God.

May we also be convinced that the physical and moral health of the family and of society can be saved, protected and strengthened only by a generous obedience to Your laws.

And what about peace of mind and heart? A woman spoke at table in front of her husband and a priest friend: "Twenty-five years ago I had an abortion, and after that I have never had a day of peace. Even now I keep confessing this sin, but I cannot forget. Why? Why?"

Although contrary to what we often hear in our day, the following story is brief but striking. A seventeen-year-old girl was on her way to an abortion clinic, determined to end the innocent life within her. Meanwhile, a close friend of hers entered a book center of the Daughters of Saint Paul, whose mission is to spread the word of God through books, pamphlets and other media. Excitedly, the young woman asked the Sisters to pray for her friend so that she would change her mind about having an abortion. "I tried to convince her not to go ahead, and urged her in every way possible. You see, I myself have had an abortion and ever since then I have had no peace of mind. I want to save her from this. Please pray, Sisters, that she'll change her mind." The immediate answer was a pamphlet on abortion and a promise of prayer. With this the girl left.

A few days later she came back, her expression of anxiety replaced by one of relief. "I reached my friend in time," she said. "Although quite reluctant, she did read your pamphlet and was very much impressed by it. She did not go through with the abortion, but returned home. And her mother assured her that she herself would care for the baby. Thank you, Sisters, for your prayers and your mission."

May all people of good will who desire to serve the true interests of the family in the world, work so that plans can be made which will permit an honest and happy family life, in which the exigencies of morality are not sacrificed to individual pleasure or to individual well-being.

May whoever wishes to erect the civic and social structure on strong and stable bases, recognize the fact, based on truth, that it can be founded only on a conception of marriage and the family which is in conformity with the order established by You, our Creator and Lord.

With your help, O Lord, we shall respect and esteem the great gift of life. Be our light and our strength as we strive to hear and make Your voice heard more clearly in the din of our confused age. Then, and only then, will we be blessed with peace of mind and countless graces.

Prayer

Jesus Master, once You said these unforgettable words to Your disciples: "You are the light of the world. A city set on a hill cannot be hidden. Men do not light a lamp and then put it under a bushel basket. They set it on a stand where it gives light to all in the house. In the same way, your light must shine before men so that they may see goodness in your acts and give praise to your heavenly Father" (Matthew 5:14-16). Make me a reflector of Your light so that those around me, beginning with my family, my relatives and friends, may find at least a little bit of You in me.

INDEX

abortion 19ff., 23, 49, 115, 131, 133, 135
absolution 49, 62
  power of 46
adoration 78, 87, 100
aged, the 27f.
amendment 51, 62
Anointing of the Sick 105-107
Apostles 32f., 44ff., 93, 109, 111
  lay 37
Augustine, St. 58, 73, 94
authority
  parental 127

Baptism 14-29, 36
  effects of 16f.
  formula of 19
  instituted by Christ 15
  necessity of 15
  of blood 22
  of desire 22
  of infants 17
Bible 28
birth control 134
bishop(s) 19, 33, 46
Blessed Sacrament
  see *Eucharist*
body 25f.

character 56
  baptismal 16
charismatics 40f.
charity 59, 101
Charles Borromeo, St. 58
child(ren) 17f., 20, 51ff., 114, 121, 126ff., 131
chrism 35
Christian(s) 36
  "born-again" 17
Church 16, 19, 28, 40, 73, 93, 95, 99
  has power to forgive sins 47
  interpreter of revelation 100
  Mystical Body of Christ 41

Communion 55, 59, 62, 77ff., 84, 86, 103
  daily reception of 101
  preparation and thanksgiving for 84
  reception under both kinds 85
concupiscence 16
confession 54, 57f., 61f.
  at least yearly 51
  frequent 59
  of children 54
  see also *Penance; Reconciliation*
confessional 63f.
confessor(s) 49, 53, 63, 65
confidence 48, 72, 106
Confirmation 31-42
  seal of 35
conscience 55
  examination of 49, 58, 62
Consecration 68, 74, 87ff., 91, 94
contrition 65
conversion 36
Council of Trent 74
cross 94, 100
Cyprian, St. 33, 46, 93
Cyril of Jerusalem, St. 74

death 16, 25f.
destiny
  of man 130
devil 31, 106
devotion
  Eucharistic 87
disabled, the 27
discipline 128
divorce 123
duties 85

education
  of children 127
  religious 122
eternity 22

138

INDEX 139

Eucharist 51, 53, 67-103, 74, 85, 95
  a sacrament and sacrifice 69, 87f.
  disrespect for 68, 80
  effects of reception of 84
  institution of 70
  prefigured in Old Testament 69
  promised in New Testament 69
  reception of 55
  true body and blood of Christ 74
  unworthy reception of 72
Eucharistic Celebration 68, 74, 77
  see also *Mass*
euthanasia 23
evangelization 36

Faith 27f., 31, 36, 40, 70, 73
faithfulness 122
family 119, 127, 130, 135,
  nucleus of society 114
fatherhood 122, 129
Fathers of the Church 48, 73
faults 56
fetus 26
fidelity 125, 133
forgiveness 46, 48
fortitude 40

General Catechetical Directory 52
generation 26
God
  Author of Matrimony 119
  eager to forgive sin 57
  Father 12
Gospel 36, 62
grace 11, 13, 15, 63, 65, 84f., 106
  actual 65
  sacramental 62
  sanctifying 13, 16, 35, 59, 65
guilt 55

heaven 65, 130
hell 51
holiness 36f.
Holy Orders 74, 109-115
Holy Spirit 28, 32, 35, 39, 41
  devotion to 40
  gifts of 13, 16, 35
  strength of 31, 35
holydays of obligation 100

human nature
  weakness of 31
human rights 22
humility 72
husband 121

Ignatius of Antioch, St. 73
immorality 114
impenitents 47
infanticide 23, 133
infants 26
  and Baptism 17, 21f.
intellect 25
Irenaeus, St. 93

Jesus Christ 20, 31, 38, 43, 45, 48, 111
  Divine Teacher 11f.
  Head of Mystical Body 84
  High Priest 95
  Mediator 89
  Mystical Body of 16
  Priest 102
  priestly role of 17, 109
  Redeemer 74, 95
  Savior 43
  the Bread of Life 70
  truly present in the Eucharist 78
  Truth 84
  union with 84
  Victim 93
John Chrysostom, St. 58
John Nepomucene, St. 57
John the Baptist, St. 43
John Vianney, St. 59
Justin Martyr, St. 73

knowledge 24

laity 36, 38f.
Last Supper 69, 73, 91f., 95
life 131ff., 136
  eternal 21
  right to 133
liturgy 94, 99
love 13, 50, 118, 120, 125, 129
  conjugal 118, 122

140 THE SACRAMENTS AND YOU

malice 48
marriage 124, 130, 276f.
  dignity and sanctity of 120
  indissolubility of 120
  see also *Matrimony*
martyrdom 22
Mary 111
  Mother of God 115
  Refuge of sinners 59
  the Mother of Jesus 32
Mass 59, 68, 74, 79, 87, 91, 93, 97ff.
  ingredients for 75ff.
  institution of 91
  nature of 94
  Tridentine Latin 98
  value of 103
Matrimony 117-136
  God as Author of 119
  grace communicated in 120ff.
  see also *marriage*
mercy 48, 106
  of God 64f.
morality 135
morals 40
motherhood 122, 129
Mystery
  Eucharistic 98

Newman, John Cardinal 56

Old Testament 43
optimism 40
ordination 110

parent(s) 18, 53, 122, 127
parenthood 127ff.
passion(s) 31, 133
Paul, St. 71f., 113f.
peace 64, 84
Penance 43, 49f., 52f., 62
  before First Communion 52
  effects of 55, 64
  good reception of 50
  liturgical celebrations of 61f.
  rite of 48
  see also *confession; Reconciliation*
penitent(s) 49f., 58, 61f., 64
Pentecost 32
Pentecostals 40f.
perfection 101

person(s) 23, 26, 130
Peter, St. 32, 43
planned parenthood 134
prayer 59
priest(s) 46ff., 49, 61, 95f., 101f., 109
  power of, to forgive sins 46f.
procreation 130
prophets 31, 43
punishment
  eternal 58
  temporal 61, 65, 84, 106

Real Presence 67f., 70
reason
  age of 52f.
Reconciliation 43-65
  see also *confession; Penance*
reconciliation 50
redemption 50
religion 39
repentance 43
resolution 50
respect
  between husband and wife 121
resurrection 45, 50
retarded, the 26f.
revelation 100

sacraments 40
  means of grace 28
  saving actions of Jesus 11
sacrifice
  Eucharist as 87-101
  of the cross 89, 94, 100
saints 65
salvation 17, 20f., 64, 88
sanctification 16
sanctity 65
scandal 62
Scripture 97
self-control 125
separation 125
sick, the 105, 107
sickness 106
sin(s) 16, 43, 47f., 51, 64, 102
  confession of 49f.
  forgiveness of 47
  mortal 44, 52, 57f., 106
  original 18
  power to forgive 44

INDEX 141

remission of 55
venial 53, 59f., 64f., 84, 106
sinner(s) 43, 57, 64
society 114, 119
sorrow 59
  imperfect 51
  perfect 50
soul(s) 25ff., 57
  in purgatory 102
spouses 127, 131
suffering 16
Sunday 100

temptation(s) 40, 43
Ten Commandments 27
Teresa of Avila, St. 18f., 49, 58
thankfulness 50
transubstantiation 69, 91
truth 13, 40

unborn, the 19

Vatican II 37f., 40, 92, 99
  changes of 97
vice 54
virtue(s) 54, 65
  cardinal 16
  theological 13, 16, 27, 35, 84
vocation
  Christian 122

wife 121
witness(es) 101
  of Christ 35f., 40
woman(en) 112ff.
  not to be ordained 110f.
Word of God 97
world 135
  spirit of the 31
worship 39, 78

Daughters of St. Paul

MASSACHUSETTS
 50 St. Paul's Ave., Jamaica Plain, Boston, MA 02130; **617-522-8911**.
 172 Tremont Street, Boston, MA 02111; **617-426-5464; 617-426-4230**.

NEW YORK
 78 Fort Place, Staten Island, NY 10301; **718-447-5071; 718-447-5086**.
 59 East 43rd Street, New York, NY 10017; **212-986-7580**.
 625 East 187th Street, Bronx, NY 10458; **212-584-0440**.
 525 Main Street, Buffalo, NY 14203; **716-847-6044**.

NEW JERSEY
 Hudson Mall—Route 440 and Communipaw Ave.,
  Jersey City, NJ 07304; **201-433-7740**.

CONNECTICUT
 202 Fairfield Ave., Bridgeport, CT 06604; **203-335-9913**.

OHIO
 2105 Ontario Street (at Prospect Ave.), Cleveland, OH 44115;
  216-621-9427.
 616 Walnut Street, Cincinnati, OH 45202; **513-421-5733; 513-721-5059**.

PENNSYLVANIA
 1719 Chestnut Street, Philadelphia, PA 19103; **215-568-2638**.

VIRGINIA
 1025 King Street, Alexandria, VA 22314; **703-683-1741; 703-549-3806**.

SOUTH CAROLINA
 243 King Street, Charleston, SC 29401; **803-577-0175**.

FLORIDA
 2700 Biscayne Blvd., Miami, FL 33137; **305-573-1618; 305-573-1624**.

LOUISIANA
 4403 Veterans Memorial Blvd., Metairie, LA 70006; **504-887-7631;
  504-887-0113**.
 423 Main Street, Baton Rouge, LA 70802; **504-343-4057; 504-381-9485**.

MISSOURI
 1001 Pine Street (at North 10th), St. Louis, MO 63101; **314-621-0346;
  314-231-1034**.

ILLINOIS
 172 North Michigan Ave., Chicago, IL 60601; **312-346-4228; 312-346-3240**.

TEXAS
 114 Main Plaza, San Antonio, TX 78205; **512-224-8101; 512-224-0938**.

CALIFORNIA
 1570 Fifth Ave., San Diego, CA 92101; **619-232-1442**.
 46 Geary Street, San Francisco, CA 94108; **415-781-5180**.

WASHINGTON
 2301 Second Ave., Seattle, WA 98121; **206-441-3300; 206-441-3210**.

HAWAII
 1143 Bishop Street, Honolulu, HI 96813; **808-521-2731**.

ALASKA
 750 West 5th Ave., Anchorage, AK 99501; **907-272-8183**.

CANADA
 3022 Dufferin Street, Toronto 395, Ontario, Canada.